MYSTERIOUS GOD

Bernard Hoose

Mysterious God

the columba press

First published in 2014 by
the columba press
55A Spruce Avenue,
Stillorgan Industrial Park,
Blackrock, County Dublin

Cover design by David Mc Namara CSsR
Origination by The Columba Press
Printed by SprintPrint Ltd

ISBN 978 1 78218 182 8

∞

A huge 'thank you' to my wife Jayne Hoose for her careful reading and constructive criticism of an earlier version of this manuscript, and for her invaluable suggestions.

∞

Contents

Introduction

This book is about knowing God. Necessarily, then, it is about knowing mystery. Now, for obvious reasons, this can seem more than a little strange. When we say that God is mystery, we mean that God is unknown and unknowable, incapable of being analysed, inexplicable, incomprehensible and, in spite of numerous efforts made by some philosophers and theologians, indefinable. Given this state of affairs, it might seem that little more could be written in a book about our mysterious God beyond what is contained in the preceding sentence. The obvious response to that, of course, is to point to what has been given to us in revelation. There is, however, a good deal more than even that to discuss. This is largely because of our need to deal with the innumerable problems we cause ourselves. At the base of most, perhaps all, of our problems in this regard is the fact that we experience enormous difficulty in accepting one of the most important points that has been revealed to us: the notion of mystery. In short, although we are usually content to *say* that God is mystery, many of us often (dare I say usually?) behave as though that were not the case.

To some extent, this book is about the mistakes we make in this regard, and how we might both avoid and overcome such errors. Beyond that, however, it is a plea to let God be God in our lives. Only when that happens can the great adventure really begin. Only when that happens does real life begin. Only when that happens do we gain any kind of awareness of what real life is. Only then, moreover, does it make sense to talk about knowing

God. In other words, in spite of everything that has been said thus far, this book really is about knowing God.

A word of warning, however, before we proceed to the first chapter. A danger that could plague a book about God as mystery is that it might be used as nothing more than a springboard for a purely intellectual exercise. At this point, some readers who are engaged in the study of spirituality at a university or other similar centre of learning may well wonder what else they are supposed to do. But let me explain. It is, of course, normal to adopt an intellectual approach to books on the various sciences, or on politics, economics, and innumerable other topics, including theology. The author of a book on economics, sociology, or whatever, sets out some ideas, and the reader uses his or her intellect to absorb, analyse, agree with, disagree with, or criticise what is written. This is a familiar and useful process, and it is one that has borne a good deal of fruit throughout the history of humankind. Where mystery is concerned, however, our intellects are simply not enough. In fact, they can all too easily get in the way. That said, there is some room for intellectual work. Readers may not, for example, agree with what I have to say on certain points. Hopefully, however, we will not get stuck at that level. We can indulge in critical analysis with some profit, but, where mystery is concerned, we also (and most importantly) do well in reaching beyond, in being open to the mystery itself, to God. And, in the main, this book is about doing just that. Where such openness comes about, I dare to suggest that the inevitable inadequacy of the writer and the inaccuracy of the words written will take on less importance, as will, if I may say so, the inevitably inadequate abilities of the reader, whoever he or she may be. The real adventure takes place in a world beyond the intellect of either of us.

As the more academically minded among my readers will soon note, I have chosen to avoid using theological jargon as much as possible, partly in order to make the book more widely accessible, and partly because, quite frankly, I do not believe that such terminology would add anything of value.

The False Gods of Christians

What is God? There are, of course, dictionary definitions and descriptions. Some of what we find in dictionaries, however, reflects notions that are peculiar to the belief systems of certain religions or ideas found in the works of particular philosophers. If we strip away the inevitable bias that is contained or reflected in these notions, what we are left with is little more than a definition of God as the Supreme Being. What, then, is the Supreme Being? Most of us, it seems, have some sort of notion – vague or otherwise – of what *we* mean when we use that term, but is that notion helpful? The fact is, whatever ideas we may have are certain to be woefully inadequate. They are probably also woefully misleading. Consider the following short narrative, which, although invented, is likely to reflect the experience of most Christians at some time, perhaps many times, during their lives.

The fair-haired man in the long, dark overcoat moved purposefully from the centre of the church to his favourite spot in a quiet little alcove on the right. Slowly and reverently he removed a book of psalms from his brief-case, opened it at the page he had marked the last time he had been there, settled himself into a kneeling position, and began to pray to the monster that he called 'God'. The monster was not, of course, some diabolical creature he had actually encountered at some stage in his life. Nor was it entirely the product of his own imagination. Numerous other people, including his parents, a few schoolteachers and one or two priests were among those who had contributed over time to the creation of this idol.

He was, however, strangely unaware of how this dangerous piece of fiction had come into being, or indeed that it was a piece of fiction. Had he been asked to identify the object of his adoration, he would have declared, without any hesitation whatsoever, that it was the God revealed by Jesus Christ.

In short, the fair-haired man would have been astonished to hear it suggested that he was praying to a monster of his own and others' making. 'My God,' he would have said, 'loves us and sent Jesus to save us'. In reality, however, this man's god is a complex mixture of divine revelation and sheer human invention – a contradictory mixture of kindness, callousness, beauty and horror. In practice, I venture to suggest, he is not unusual among humans, or even among Christians, although, perhaps very few Christians would see themselves as being within this category. They might well admit to entertaining hopelessly inadequate ideas about God, but that word 'monster' is not likely to be a term they would readily apply to those ideas. After all, it brings to mind notions of cruelty and all manner of wickedness. Of course, we are all aware that, in times past, cruelty was an aspect of many attempts to keep the Church 'pure'. We are also aware that such cruelty was often exerted by people holding positions of authority within the Church, and that many such authority figures claimed to be acting on behalf of God. Nowadays, however, although intolerance is still a common enough feature of much that is called Christian, it is not usually expressed as violently as it was in some earlier centuries. Many followers of Christ, moreover, are far from intolerant and certainly do not think of God as being so. In this sense, then, it would seem that they can fairly be said not to believe in a monstrous God. The word 'monster', however, can be applied in other ways. It can, for instance, simply be applied to an imaginary being which has human or animal features, and is, in some sense, ugly. It is difficult, perhaps impossible, for us to conceive of God in a way that does not include some human and, therefore, purely imaginary aspects. Given this state of affairs, the fact is that, although we may not think of God as being ugly, any conception we have will necessarily be appallingly deficient in beauty, goodness and, indeed, love. Although many – most of us, I imagine – would claim not to envisage God as monstrous in the cruel and wicked sense of the word, it is normal for there to be a good deal of invention in just about everybody's conception of the Supreme Being. Indeed, this is so even in cases in which, on the whole, God is seen as loving. In short, probably all those who believe in God feel the need for some sort of image (visual or otherwise) of the being on whom they pin their deepest hopes and desires. The fact is, however, that God is beyond the limits of anything that we can think about or imagine.

Although this truth is immensely important, it seems unlikely that most of us will be able to change our ways in this regard very quickly and, in spite of all that has been said above, perhaps we should not concern ourselves very much with trying to do so. After all, many of us have found that, in spite of their inevitable imperfections, our imaginings can aid our meditations and also give some sort of focus to our vocal prayer. If, of course, we move into the realm of contemplation, which we shall discuss later, things will change, and imaginings will disappear. Until that happens, however, what is important is that we always keep in mind the fact that anything we imagine or think about God is always going to be totally inadequate. The really dangerous thing is not that we might go on forming images which could aid prayer and meditation, but that we might go on trying to limit God to those inadequate images and our own little ideas about the divine. Problems of some kind are always likely to arise as a result of such a process simply because we find it hard not to become attached to our own ideas and imaginings. As a result, we may, for instance, be slow to appreciate other people's spiritual insights at times, merely because such appreciation would require inconvenient and perhaps disturbing modification of our own notions about God. Problems of a much more serious kind arise when people become convinced that their conception of God, or the one that other people have pushed into their minds, is absolute truth, and that anything else is a lie. A glance at the history of the Church indicates that such has been the case on numerous occasions during the last two millennia. When this happens, our conceptions can acquire immense and even dangerous power – power to close our eyes and ears to the good news of Jesus Christ when it is set before us.

Most of those who do *not* believe in God probably also feel the need to have an image of what it is that they reject. They may or may not have mental pictures of this being, but they must surely have some concept in mind. If this were not the case, what sense would there be in any declaration on their part that they do not believe in God? Bearing this in mind, we can see that, in discussions with atheists, we need to ask them what they are referring to when they use the word 'God'. In reply, some of them may well say that they reject all gods of all religions. Such a response would have validity, however, only if those giving it were capable of knowing all the possible concepts that people could have in mind when they used the word 'god', with or without a capital 'G'. Clearly, that is impossible. Many atheists, one suspects, have in mind a god that has been conveyed to them in some way through their contact with people who do declare a belief in a god. What they reject, it would seem, is that particular god (or, at least, what they have come to understand about that god), and it could well be the case that some atheists have in mind not just one but various gods and various kinds of gods that have been mentioned in conversation or in writing by various believers. All of those gods, of course, could be monstrous in the cruel and wicked sense mentioned above, and one suspects that, in some way or other, the gods that atheists have in mind are always quite bad.

In recent times, a poster appeared on the sides of London buses declaring that God probably does not exist and people should therefore stop worrying and enjoy themselves. Clearly, those responsible for this poster had an ogre in mind when they referred to 'God'. Why else should believers be consumed with worry and not enjoy themselves? Those who have really heard the good news of Jesus Christ should have no difficulty in agreeing with atheists that such a god does not exist. Indeed they should also have no difficulty in agreeing that some other, less malign, 'old man in the sky' type gods do not exist. Saying this, of course, is very different from saying that God does not exist. It does seem to be the case, however, that many who call themselves Christians do appear to believe in an almighty ogre. Students of Church history, moreover, soon find that this has long been the case. Given this state of affairs, it seems hardly surprising that, for a long time, God was portrayed by one group of Christians as approving of the appalling cruelty inflicted by Protestants during the Reformation period, and, by another group, as approving of the appalling cruelty inflicted by Roman Catholics during the same period. Much earlier, God had been portrayed as approving of, and even willing, a number of so-called holy wars (or Crusades). All of this, of course, happened a long time ago. We should, however, be wary of having feelings of satisfaction merely because any inadequate and misleading ideas about God to which we cling – our false gods, if you like – appear not to have produced anything quite so catastrophic in recent times. They are still problematic if they are obstacles in our spiritual lives.

But what about revelation?
Some people will perhaps be inclined to claim that the only ideas they have about God are those that have been given to us in revelation. The fact is, however, that we tend to put our own slant on revelation. We have our own interpretation of it. It is hard to avoid this. Anything we read is read in the light of our experiences and of ideas that we have already formed. As we shall see later, even a conviction that God is love may not be completely devoid of problems. Much depends upon what we mean by love, and what we mean by that word is always going to result from our own experience and education. In short, if we are to make progress spiritually, it is important for us to be always aware that God, and love of the kind that Jesus discusses, are beyond anything that we are capable of thinking about the divine.

Mystery and attempts to explain it

What we really need to do is wake up to the fact of mystery. Unfortunately, even within Christian circles, there is sometimes confusion about the meaning of this term in its association with God, and it is not difficult to ascertain how some of that confusion has come about. At times, for instance, the word 'mystery' was associated with religions which had teachings that were hidden from the majority of people. Indeed, it was often the case that only certain members were initiated into those secrets. Such religions are often referred to as 'mystery religions' because of this secret or hidden 'wisdom'. A not entirely different source of confusion, however, is found much closer to home. Within Christianity itself, the impression is sometimes conveyed that the Gospel is far from simple, and only those who have studied long and hard at a theological college or university can begin to grapple with its intricacies. Such people are portrayed as being in some way closer to the secrets than the not so well read. There is, however, no sound reason for thinking this is the case. God is beyond the boundaries of our understanding. No amount of study can change that simple fact.

Nevertheless, a glance at the history of the Church shows that it has not always been easy for Christians to accept the limits of their intellectual abilities. This becomes obvious when we consider the fact that, over the centuries, numerous versions of the mystery have appeared in Christian literature. In other words, there have been many different 'explanations' of what cannot be explained. This is, of course, very strange to relate, but that is how things are. In fact, the lack of unity among the followers of Christ is largely, although not entirely, explained by the very fact that, at certain times, certain Christians claimed knowledge which they simply could not have. It is true, of course, that many of the causes of division among Christians are not specifically disagreements about God. There is also disagreement, for instance, about the morality of various kinds of activity; about attitudes to Mary, the mother of Jesus; about when, if ever, divorce is possible for Christians; and about whether or not certain books and sections of other books should be accepted as parts of the Bible. Over the course of the last two millennia, however, there has also been disagreement about God's attitude to various matters; about God's plans; about what we might perhaps call God's character; and, indeed, about the inner life of God. Thus we find, for example, that a good deal of ink has been spilt and a good deal of division has ensued concerning whether or not God has predestined some of us for eternal life and some for eternal damnation. Various attempts at explaining – and even defining – how the second person of the Trinity is present in the Eucharistic celebration have also contributed to serious divisions among Christians, as have attempts to explain the relationship between the Holy Spirit and the other two members of the Trinity. Other examples abound. Clearly it would be a mistake to suggest that this is merely a problem of the past. In short, no matter what we may say and even believe to be the case, most of us, it appears, experience a good deal of difficulty in taking seriously the notion of God as mystery. Instead we try to define the unknowable and explain even the inner workings of the inexplicable.

It is important to take note of this because the ideas that we have about God affect our way of looking at the world, and, conversely, our way of looking at the world affects our ideas about God. Of course, world views (and ideas about what God will allow within those visions of the world) vary enormously. Some, being very restrictive, are productive of complex lists of rules. Others are astonishingly permissive, and some have even been supportive of the most atrocious violence and cruelty, as was noted above in reference to the Crusades. Often we find complex lists of rules and permissiveness together. This seems to have been the case for large numbers of people both during and for some time after the period known as the Reformation. Rigid, rule-bound thinking was accompanied by violent enforcement of those rules, and God, it was claimed, approved of the rules while permitting the cruelty. At times, people judged to be heretics were executed, and, bizarrely, those doing the judging about heresy in each of the churches that were involved in such activity were themselves regarded as heretics in other churches. All sides, of course, claimed to be doing God's will. In short, it seems that different versions of the divine permitted different assassinations. I imagine that few, if any, Christians today would even countenance the thought that God would be in favour of such intolerance and cruelty. At the same time, however, it does seem that there is a pretty common tendency to try to force God, or at least our idea of God, into our world view, or else to adapt our view of the world to the all-too-human god that our intellects and imaginations have produced – even if we are fairly tolerant of the points of view of other people. It may seem strange to suggest that something similar is found even among atheists, but a little reflection suffices to show that particular kinds of vision of the world would necessitate the rejection of certain types of god. In short, we have a tendency to live in a world of our own making. If, however, we wish to encounter reality, we have to step into mystery.

Mystery and our desire to control

Stepping into mystery amounts to coming home. Ruth Burrows puts it like this when discussing the notion of the hiddenness of God in the writings of the Spanish mystic, John of the Cross:

> We ourselves are mystery and our proper ambience is mystery. When we speak of God's hiddenness we are saying he is the answer to our yearning. He is unfathomable mystery offered to us. Through Jesus he reveals himself not only as our beloved – the object of desire – but as our lover. Then we realize that he has always been our beloved for the simple reason that he *is* our lover. We learn that here is a fulfilment to our endless longing but not within ourselves, not within the limitations of this world or our own achievements, but as pure gift.
>
> (Burrows, pp. 20–1. Emphasis hers)

Unfortunately, it seems that it is not easy for us to readily embrace such realisation and such learning. 'There is,' says Burrows, 'an inevitable conflict between our true self and its deepest desire to be enfolded, possessed by our beloved, and the innate drive to control, possess, to find fulfilment within ourselves, of ourselves' (Burrows, p. 21). This conflict, it seems to me, lies at the heart of many of our problems – perhaps, in one way or another, all of them. Any lack of awareness on our part of just how wide ranging this conflict is can easily be explained by the fact that the innate drive to control and possess expresses itself in complex ways. As we might expect, some of those who forcefully experience this innate drive to control and possess are inclined to reject God. They do not come to this way of thinking, of course, as a result of becoming convinced that, in the absence of God, humans are capable of controlling all situations and avoiding all disasters. That would be madness. Rather, it seems, they are simply inclined to reject that which does not fit into their world view, and, of course, if there is no place for God (or what they consider God to be) in their world view, God has to be rejected. As is probably the case with just about all of us, their vision of things is, for them, a precious possession, and they want to have some control over it. In other words, it seems that they hanker not so much for control of the world as for control of their *view* of that world. In fairness, we should note the likelihood that, in most such cases, at least a part of the world view of people who reject God has been influenced by meeting with or hearing of people who believe in a god that is eminently refutable.

The drive to control and possess, however, is also found among believers, and it propels them into trying to control God – although they might never admit as much, even to themselves. Needless to say, what is controlled in practice is not God at all, but rather a product of their own thoughts and imaginations, and such attempted control is, of course, a mere intellectual exercise. Those who indulge in it try to make God fit into the way they see things, the way they think about things. Perhaps all believers fall into this trap at some stage in their lives. God, however, cannot be contained within the intellectual processes of human beings. The realisation that we cannot 'think God' was addressed head on in *The Cloud of Unknowing*, a highly influential spiritual text written in England during the fourteenth century. Although it has been widely read, the impression one gains upon reading it is that the book was originally written specifically for just one of the anonymous author's disciples. God, the young reader is told, cannot be grasped by means of a thinking process. Only through love can we come to the divine. Between us and God, says the author, is a cloud of unknowing, which he also describes in terms of a darkness that prevents us from seeing God through the light of reason. Any experience of God we may have in this life will always be in this cloud and darkness (*The Cloud of Unknowing*, p. 22).

> But now you ask me, 'How am I to think of God himself, and what is he?' And to this I can only answer, 'I do not know'.
>
> For with your question you have brought me into that very darkness and that very cloud of unknowing that I want you to be in yourself. By grace it is possible to have full knowledge of all other created things and their works, and indeed of the works of God himself, and to think clearly about them, but of God himself no one can think. And so I wish to give up everything that I can think, and choose as my love the one thing that I cannot think. For he can well be loved, but he cannot be thought. By love he can be grasped and held, but by thought neither grasped nor held.
>
> (*Cloud*, pp. 27–8)

Mention of the fact that we can know God's works but not know what God is, or indeed how to think about God, may well have caused a question or two to arise in the minds of many of those who have read *The Cloud of Unknowing*. After all, does not St Paul say that what can be known about God is plain to see? And does he not also say that the deity and eternal power of God have always been clearly perceived in creation (Rom 1:19–20)? This, however, is the same Paul who says that our knowledge and prophecy are imperfect. Now we see without clarity and we know only in part (1 Cor 13:8–12). The peace of God, which, he tells us, will guard our hearts and our thoughts, is beyond our under-standing (Phil 4:7). There is no contradiction between, on the one hand, declaring that awareness of God can be gained through experience and reflection upon creation, and on the other hand, declaring that God is beyond our understanding. In short, it seems that, as Paul sees things, although we can become aware of the Supreme Being and, in some mysterious way, we can become aware that this is the source of everything that is true, just, lovable and admirable, there is little else we can know about God in this life. Saying that we can gain awareness of the loving God in the manner described by Paul is very different from saying that the human intellect can grasp God in a concept. It is, of course, important in this life to know things – to know, for instance, that certain foods are good for us while others are bad; that certain kinds of behaviour are likely to damage the ecosystem; that learning to read can open up many possibilities for us and so on. Similarly, we need to know that God is mystery. However, it is also useful to know that, because of our conditioning and our longing for certainty, even the word 'God' can be a source of problems for us. Almost inevitably, it carries along with itself whatever corrupt images and thoughts about the divine each of us may have. It tends to denote what we think the Supreme Being is, and the simple fact is that we do not know what the Supreme Being is, even if we have awareness that this Being is the source of everything that is lovely. It is indeed important to know many things, and one of the most important is the fact that our ability to know is limited.

The anonymous author of *The Cloud of Unknowing* was certainly not the first Christian to write about the futility of trying to think God. In fact, he shows awareness of this in expressing approval of the writings of a much earlier author whom he calls St Denys, but who is now known as Pseudo-Dionysius. This latter's works appear to have been written late in the fifth century or early in the sixth. Of particular significance for our present discussion is the fact that, in a very short work entitled *Mystical Theology*, Pseudo-Dionysius talks about mystics being plunged into the darkness of unknowing. Enclosed within this darkness, and with their reasoning powers inactive, they are united to what is wholly unknowable. Through knowing nothing, he says, they know what is beyond their knowledge (Pseudo-Dionysius, ch. 1).

All this talk about clouds and darkness, however, is not without problems of its own. In order that we might understand things more easily and, indeed, more deeply than would otherwise be the case, we often make use of metaphors. Jesus, for instance, is often referred to as a shepherd. In fact, in St John's Gospel, he is portrayed describing himself as such. This kind of language can, of course, help people who are reading or listening to gain a deeper understanding of what is being discussed than might otherwise be the case. Such deeper understanding is likely to come about, however, only if those readers or listeners bear in mind the limits that need to be applied. If they forget or ignore those limits, problems may arise. Real shepherds, for instance, herd sheep. Although there seems to be little danger of Christians thinking that Jesus really was a shepherd in this literal sense, the history of applying the term also to bishops, priests and other ministers of religion has sometimes had unfortunate side effects, with the people whom they served sometimes being treated, it appears, rather like unintelligent woolly animals. In short, it seems that we sometimes forget that metaphors really are only metaphors. We know that they are not to be understood literally, but, in spite of that, we sometimes apply them in ways that were not intended by their original users.

Even when we are aware of this danger we can still run into difficulties because of our almost automatic tendency to form a picture of the chosen metaphor, at least vaguely, in our imagination. Even the use of an apparently simple metaphor like a cloud or darkness can be problematic if we take to imagining clouds and darkness. For many of us, I venture to suggest, it is extremely difficult not to do so. Recognising this danger, the author of *The Cloud of Unknowing* spells out the fact that, when he refers to 'darkness', he is talking about an absence of knowing. What we do not know is, in a sense, dark to us – we cannot see it with our mind's eye (*Cloud*, p. 26).[1] Pseudo-Dionysius, on the other hand, tries to clarify things by further complicating his use of metaphors. He prays that divine wisdom will guide us to the summit of mystical knowledge, where the mysteries of theology outshine every kind of brilliance 'with the intensity of their darkness'. This could seem odd. What he refers to as 'darkness' here, however, could alternatively be described as far too much light. Both darkness and excessive light blind us. Whichever description we use, however, is still only a metaphor – something to help us get some sort of crude handle on the notion that, where God is concerned, we are dealing with mystery. Our intellects, Pseudo-Dionysius goes on to say, are blinded by the invisible beauty of glories which surpass all beauty (Pseudo-Dionysius, ch. 1). Further on in the same work, he prays that we may reach this darkness, which he describes as being beyond light, and that, without either seeing or knowing, we may see and know what is 'above vision and knowledge through the realisation that by not-seeing and by unknowing we attain to true vision and knowledge' (Pseudo-Dionysius, ch. 2).

Writing even earlier than Pseudo-Dionysius, Gregory of Nyssa speaks about the same things in a slightly different way. As we approach contemplation, he says, we leave behind what is communicated to us by our senses and also what our intelligence thinks it sees. Eventually, we come upon what is invisible and incomprehensible, and there we see God.

> This is the true knowledge of what is sought; this is the seeing that consists in not seeing, because that which is sought transcends all knowledge, being separated on all sides by incomprehensibility as by a kind of darkness. Wherefore John the Sublime, who penetrated into the luminous darkness, says, 'No one has ever seen God' [John 1:18], thus asserting that knowledge of the divine essence is unattainable …
>
> (Gregory of Nyssa, pp. 80–1)

What are we to make of all this, then? It may seem at first sight that, where our basic attitude to God is concerned, most of us are far from where we should be and, indeed, that we are incapable of changing our ways. In reality, however, what Gregory, Pseudo-Dionysius and the author of *The Cloud of Unknowing* have to say on these matters is not as foreign to us as we may at first believe.

Burrows points out that, in reality, our longing for what we cannot understand is deeper than any desire that we may have for knowledge or what we might normally call 'experience'. We simply do not want mystery to give way to intellectual clarity (Burrows, p. 20). This, I think, is true. It may well be difficult for us to resist the temptation to exaggerate the capacity of our intellect, but it is far from impossible for us to do so. Strange though it may seem, we are capable of reaching beyond our intellects, and it is in such reaching beyond that we can become aware of a different kind of knowing – a knowing beyond knowing. As we have just seen, this kind of knowing is mentioned by Pseudo-Dionysius. The author of *The Cloud of Unknowing* also talks about knowing through love. This will be discussed in a later chapter. Before entering into such discussion, however, we first need to take a look at a number of problems that arise in the sphere of religion, and which can all too easily throw us off course.

Chapter Two

Mystery and Problems in Religion

What exactly is religion? Various attempts have been made to explain the origin of the word, or at least the origin of the Latin word *religio*. One that we find mentioned by the early Christian writers Lactantius and St Augustine links the word to the Latin verb *religare*, which means 'to tie' or 'to bind'. God and human beings are thus seen as bound together. This explanation of the word's origin is disputed in the world of etymology, but that is of little importance for our discussion. Whatever may or may not have been the actual history of the term, surely religion *ought* to be about links with the Supreme Being, or about the re-establishment of such links. If it is not about this, there seems to be little sense in its existence. The fact remains, however, that much of what we call 'religion' purports to fit that description – or something very like it – but, in reality, is little more than ideas and practices invented by human beings. Moreover, the preservation of the religion can so easily become the most important issue. When this happens in Christian circles, the good news of Jesus Christ takes second place behind the institution. In regard to this, Bishop John Heaps observes that:

> When religion becomes an end in itself, gathering political power so as to have its own way, it becomes a force not for full life and freedom, but for the enslaving of minds and even bodies. State religions which favor their adherents in the community and

discriminate against outsiders are not the legitimate instruments of God. The minority groups thus inhibited in their freedom can also be reinforced in their own separateness. This very separateness can become a focus of power. As both parties draw their strength and their support from their religion, adherence to the group grows stronger and separation and differences are more clearly defined. Neither the condition of the majority group nor that of the minority has any necessary connection with the Spirit of God.

(Heaps, p. 13).

We could add that, in recent times, other problems have arisen as a result of the tendency to treat religions as ends in themselves. On numerous occasions, defence of an institutionalised religion or denomination appears to have been regarded by some as more important than the protection of children and other vulnerable people who were either harmed or in serious danger of being harmed by holders of office within the religion or denomination. Any god portrayed as willing this kind of thing is certainly not God. Again we encounter obstacles to the truth, to mystery, from within the institutions.

Passing on good news or bad news
Some such obstacles have proved at times to be enormously powerful in their ability to mislead. In developing his or her own image of God, nobody, it seems, acts alone. At various stages in our lives, most of us probably received a good deal of invented stuff about the divine, including, in many cases, some very false and therefore bad news, from other members of the religious group to which we belonged. To say this is, of course, by no means to say or even hint that the churches have totally failed in their mission. The good news of Jesus Christ has been transmitted from generation to generation, and indeed to us, through the efforts of church members working under the inspiration of the Holy Spirit. There is, however, a major problem which Christian denominations have

shared with other religions. That is the problem, already noted, of allowing human invention to get in the way of what is truly important. Heaps refers to this in stark terms:

> If we are to go forward as the holy people of God, the Mystical Body of Christ and the Sacrament of salvation for the world, we must pay attention to the things essential to the faith and the teachings of Jesus and leave behind man-made structures and laws which have either outlived their purpose of being servants of the Gospel, or which in fact never really served the Gospel, but arose from an inadequate perspective of the beauty and dignity of what God has created and what Jesus renewed.
>
> (Heaps, p. 108)

A great deal of what is usually presented as religion is in practice little more than hypotheses, conjectures and contentions, as well as claims about a supposed need to cling to those hypotheses, conjectures and contentions. As such, religion can be most unattractive and stultifying. Given this state of affairs individual adherents may understandably experience difficulty in distinguishing the real pearls of revelation from the trash that bad religion places alongside those pearls. The problem is magnified by a confusing use of language. Richard Rohr refers to this in noting how religion can use the right words when teaching, for instance, that God is love. The god that is actually presented, however, is never permitted to be as loving as even what Rohr refers to as 'our middle range friends'. The means preferred by this god for bringing about transformation in us, appear to be coercion, blame, mandates and shame. Rohr says he understands that this sort of thing can be useful for social order and for controlling immature people. It is clear to him as he gets older, however, that God's love for him does not depend upon his changing. Rather, God loves him in order that he can change. He is convinced, he says, that:

> Religion, in its common cultural and external forms, largely protects the ego, especially the group ego, instead of transforming

it. If people do not go beyond first level metaphors, rituals, and comprehension, most religions seem to end up with a God who is often angry, petulant, needy, jealous, and who will love us only if we are 'worthy' and belonging to the correct group.

We have come to a strange state of affairs, says Rohr, in which we find that we ourselves are more loving, or at least striving to be more loving, than the god in whom we claim to believe:

Most people I know can eventually forgive and forget. But not our god! God does not forgive until he or she gets some appropriate penance, reparation and repayment … This is supposedly needed by one who has nothing better to do than keep accounts and do a self-centered cost analysis on everything. Sort of like Santa Claus, 'making a list and checking it twice, going to find out who's naughty or nice'. The Lord of this beautiful and self-renewing cosmos ends up looking instead like an anal retentive banker or a brooding maiden aunt. It just doesn't match the cosmic evidence. And it particularly does not match the evidence for those who have prayed – or experienced divine forgiveness.

(Rohr, 2006, pp. 3–4)

The problems to which Rohr refers are clearly not confined to religions that are labelled as 'Christian'. Our discussion, however, concerns only this last mentioned group. The ugliness and inauthenticity of their own situation notwithstanding, most adherents of such kinds of 'Christianity' seem to have little difficulty in deciding there is a good deal that is inauthentic, indeed invented, in other religions, especially, perhaps, those which do not come under the Abrahamic label.[2] Convinced, as so many of us are, about the authenticity of our own private – and even sometimes monstrous – divinities, or of the idols conveyed to our imaginations by other people within our religious groups, we often tend to look upon the gods of other religions as in some way inferior. The important thing to note here is not that we may think of these gods as inferior to God, but that, in reality, we may think of them as inferior to our own private (and inevitably crude) notions about God. Take the example of sun worshippers from several thousand years ago. Worshipping a star may strike us as primitive and way off the mark. Surely what is really important, however, is whether or not those people were, in the depths of their being, trying to rise to the transcendent. The fact that they might have thought the sun *was* the transcendent being or perhaps a manifestation of the Supreme Being is understandable, and does not necessarily mean that *all* their efforts were in vain. I am not suggesting that we examine the practices of any particular group of sun worshippers which actually existed in some place at some time. I doubt very much that any of us – specialist scholars included – knows enough about the people concerned to be able to avoid the likelihood of an interminable debate about their good and bad points. All I am suggesting is the possibility that, in some way or other, some people who worshipped the sun really did manage to get in touch with God – or rather allowed God to get in touch with them – and to rise above the mess of this world. In short, it is perfectly feasible that the sun did not prove to be quite the obstacle to divine encounter that we may have supposed it to be. We can easily miss the point here if we get distracted by far from elevating stories we have heard about morally questionable activities which may have been listed among the requirements of particular religions that involved sun worship. Even if we suppose that such activities were very common, it is still possible that some among those sun worshippers were sincerely seeking the transcendent, and, of course, we should always remember that the Holy Spirit blows where the Holy Spirit wills.

The same Holy Spirit helps us to reach beyond our own images, just as at least some sun worshippers may well have been enabled to reach beyond their small concepts. A glance at the history of the Church reveals to us, however, that the damaging images of God which Christians had at certain times proved to be more problematic than the sun. They were presented as ultimate truth, and many Christians, it seems, believed, claimed and insisted that those images were the God of Jesus Christ. Indeed petty, petulant, needy and jealous looking works of fiction have often been presented to the world as love itself. We need only think of how

God has been presented so often as an enthusiast for war, a supporter of religious intolerance and a condemning judge who is willing to punish severely even very slight misdemeanours. Small wonder then, that so many people in our time turn their backs on religion in general and on Christianity in particular, blaming it for many of the problems that exist in our world. The fact is, of course, that numerous appalling military campaigns have been conducted under the banner of religion, and, all too often, that banner has had a Christian name or symbol on it. Wars, moreover, are far from being the only horrors that have been brought about in the name of Christ and his teachings. The Gospel of love and peace has often been portrayed as having little to do with either love or peace. Over the course of several centuries, for instance, huge numbers of people, mostly women, were cruelly burned as witches. There may well have been a diabolical element among those proceedings, but probably not, it would seem, in the victims on the pyres. The Jesuit Frederick von Spee was among those who protested at this madness, but the voice of sanity, the voice of love, seems not to have been heard by those who could put a stop to the holocaust until long after von Spee's death. Moreover, when the renowned Dutch humanist Erasmus, the French Protestant theologian Sebastien Castellio, and numerous other people strongly opposed the violently expressed intolerance of many other Christians during the Reformation period, their voices too were drowned out. Over the centuries, torture, murder, theft, kidnapping, enslavement, and a whole host of other atrocities have all been performed and encouraged by Christians in the name of God, but only the invented monstrous idols of those same Christians could really have demanded such insanity.

Discovering what has value
In practice, it can be extremely difficult to avoid false gods. One imagines that this is immediately clear to most Christians when the term 'false gods' is used to refer to things which they readily see to be obstacles in the spiritual life. They see that these things

are, or can be, obstacles because they are aware of a pretty common human tendency to seek from them what can be satisfied only by God. Thus, although many of us devote a good deal of our time to pursuing such things as money, power, worldly ambitions and pleasures of various kinds, most of us are at least vaguely aware of the ability these things have to occupy places in our lives which should be occupied only by God. As a result of this, we often refer to at least some of these things as idols. These, however, are not the monstrous gods to which Rohr refers, and which are our principal concern here. What we are concerned with are gods that we really refer to as 'God' and, indeed, mistake for God. Clearly, they are not merely present in our minds. They are in the very structures of societies and religious organisations to which we belong. They infect systems and cultures, and, through a process of conditioning, can even acquire the ability to make us feel guilty if we do not do what we have been told they demand, and such conditioning can be extremely problematic.

Unfortunately, conditioning and education are hard to separate, and that is problematic because it would surely be foolish not to appreciate the benefits of a good education. While acknowledging the importance of learning, however, we also need to bear in mind the fact that not everything we habitually call education is good. The conditioning referred to above, for instance, can often come from widespread faulty education. Addressing the relevance of this for spirituality, Anthony de Mello writes: 'As one man said, "I got a pretty good education. It took me years to get over it." That's what spirituality is all about, you know: unlearning. Unlearning all the rubbish they taught you' (de Mello, p. 79). It seems that we all go through the process of learning a good deal of rubbish (along with the more useful stuff), although, undoubtedly, the amount and type of rubbish learned varies enormously from one person to another. Sometimes the imprint of the rubbish is reinforced at the very time that other people are trying to free us from it. There is nothing really surprising about this. We only ever hear what we are prepared to hear (or what others have prepared us to hear), and, for all sorts of reasons, we are not always ready for freedom and the truth that can come with it.

Our fear of release from slavery

A reluctance to accept freedom seems to be largely explained by our fear of change. If a person has always been enslaved in some way, a decision to accept freedom necessarily involves embracing change, and a fear of change, in some guise or other, seems to be almost universal. 'Better the devil you know than the devil you don't' is an expression which well portrays this aspect of the human condition. However, in some cases, the 'devil' that is labelled 'unknown' is, in fact, known to be not at all devilish. The problem it poses for us seems to have something to do with the mere fact that it is different. We are often afraid to step away from what we have here and now into a zone that we have not hitherto experienced, a zone that makes us feel decidedly uncomfortable. No surprise, then, that we cling to our cherished images of and ideas about God, even though they enslave us.

De Mello goes so far as to suggest that we hate what we fear (de Mello, p. 117). Whatever reservations some people may have about using the word 'hate' in this context, we can surely say that, generally speaking, we tend not to be at all fond of what we fear. Hence, perhaps, our willingness to use words like 'devil' when our fear of change comes to the fore. It is certainly also the case, of course, that we do like some amount of difference, some variety in our lives. Even certain kinds of major change are acceptable to us. Leaving aside the sphere of religion for a moment, we can see, for instance, that many people eagerly seize upon new electronic inventions which promise to 'revolutionise' their lives and, of course, most of us tend to welcome what we see to be changes for the better in medicine when they arrive on the scene. Nevertheless, the fact remains that most of us are loathe to be shaken out of what we see to be our comfort zones. Where these are concerned, we are afraid of losing what we have and of taking on what we do not know. This, it seems, is particularly the case where our ideas about God are concerned. Hence the intolerance that has reared its head from time to time within Christianity when opposing (or perhaps we should simply say 'different') views about the divine have been expressed. We seek certainty and security, and sometimes manage to fool ourselves into thinking that we really do have a certain amount of access to them already.

Some seekers of certainty cling to ideologies of a political nature, while others will not abide discussion of any idea that appears to challenge the scientific school of thought which has hitherto provided them with feelings of security, even when the challenge to it comes from a new school of thought which adopts a thoroughly scientific approach. In their religious thought, humans are just as susceptible to the allure of mere suppositions as they are in the sphere of politics, and, when sufficiently conditioned, just as liable to trust those suppositions as they are to trust conclusions of scientific research.

A pretty common feature in religions is the presence of a minority of people who are willing to supply these suppositions. What may occur more commonly, however, is that there is a minority of people within the religion or denomination of that religion who, having themselves been psychologically conditioned into accepting the suppositions supplied by teachers of an earlier generation, now take on the role of teachers. They teach what they have received. Referring specifically to Christian groups, one hopes, of course, that at least some of what such teachers receive is divine revelation, but what I am referring to here is their reception or inheritance of what we might call the 'add-ons' – those conjectures, hypotheses, contentions and questionable practices referred to above. It is not uncommon, moreover, for such teachers to add one or two suppositions of their own.

Another pretty common feature in religions is the presence of a majority who are more than willing to latch on to this 'certainty' that is presented to them by the minority. As will be evident from what has just been said, however, it can be misleading merely to talk about a minority and a majority. In practice, members of the minority are usually also members of the conditioned majority (perhaps we should say 'the conditioned whole'), even if some of them manage to add one or two suppositions of their own to the list of 'truths' that they inherit. All too often, we might say, the psychologically conditioned lead the psychologically conditioned.

Sinful situations, structures and cultures

There is no reason for us to be judgmental in this regard. A good deal of the misleading information we pick up about God – what de Mello calls rubbish – comes to us through the efforts of good people in our various denominations who act with sincerity of heart. It really is extremely hard – perhaps impossible in this life – to totally avoid this kind of thing. The problems are multiplied, however, when, whatever its original source may have been, a misleading or downright wrong teaching is institutionalised. Even this may come about occasionally as a result of simple error on the part of sincere people. Sometimes, however, we find ourselves confronted by what a number of theologians in recent times have called sinful structures.

Sin, of course, is essentially personal. Often, however, bad structures, systems and cultural phenomena, initially provoked by the wrongful actions of some person or persons, and added to over time by numerous others, become part of our 'normal' world and negatively affect our ability to see that something is wrong. Leaving aside for a moment the world of religion, it is not difficult to imagine, for example, how someone who is born into a society in which slavery is an integral part of daily life might not notice the wrongness of the system, even if it is obvious to visitors from other countries in which slavery does not exist. This is more likely to be the case if the slaves are well fed and no violence is used against them. Similar comments can be made about situations in which women are treated, at best, as second-class citizens. Copious other examples can be found in history books and by glancing around our world today. In short, when such sinful structures, systems and cultural phenomena are well established, many of us, it seems, suffer from moral blindness in the spheres of life that are negatively affected by them, although other people looking at our situation from outside may well see the wrongness very clearly.

Some of those bad structures may already have existed and been commonly accepted long before we were born. In such cases, because they are an integral part of our culture, it may be difficult for many of us to notice how bad they are. Indeed, a disturbing quality of some such evils is their ability to acquire invisibility.

This has been one of the discoveries of recent investigation into organisations in which there is what has come to be called institutionalised racism or institutionalised sexism. Strange though it may seem, it can even be the case that many, perhaps even all the members of such organisations are neither racist nor sexist. The institutionalised nature of the evil is such that those within the organisations do not see it. Perhaps, for instance, no one has noticed the structures that were set up a long time ago and which no one has since thought of changing make it extremely difficult for certain categories of people to hold positions of influence within the organisations concerned, or perhaps even to become members of those organisations.

Turning back to the specifically religious sphere, and even more so to the history of Christianity, we find situations of sin in which appalling acts committed in the name of God came to be viewed as acceptable by authority figures within the churches. Such was the case, for instance, in regard to the execution of so-called heretics and witches on the part of both Roman Catholics and Protestants by burning them at the stake, or by the more complex but equally barbaric procedure of hanging, drawing and quartering. Claims about God's will were also used at times by authority figures in various churches to 'justify' such horrors as torture, the enslavement of non-Christians, and clearly unjusti-fiable wars. Some such situations lasted for very long periods of time, in spite of the fact that often, perhaps always, there were people living within those very situations who were capable of seeing through the fog – as was the case with von Spee, concerning the burning of witches, and Erasmus and Castellio, concerning religious intolerance. Indeed, particularly bad situations and structures of sin can and have been known to last for hundreds of years.

Even though some of the examples so far mentioned in this chapter have since disappeared in whole or in part, it is important to remember that situations of sin exist in every generation. At any one point in time different ones may exist in different places or among different groups of people. The fact that some or even most of us do not see them is certainly no guarantee that they do not exist. Even when sinful structures and situations are pointed out to people, their conditioning and reticence to disturb their comfort zones can make them quite defensive in regard to just about any aspect of their national or local culture or, indeed, the culture of any organisation to which they belong, if they feel a strong enough affiliation to it. Bearing this in mind, it is easy for us to see how sinful structures and cultures within the religions or denominations to which people belong can play a major role in the development of misleading ideas about God, and any such hypotheses are, of course, always obstacles to openness to mystery.

Chapter Three

Uncovering the Hidden Message

In our time, a notable consequence of bad religion and the misleading ideas about God that it has promoted has been the fact that many of the words associated with religious practice (Christian or otherwise) have become decidedly unattractive to a lot of people, even to many of those who believe in God and, indeed, pray to God. Words like 'pious', 'piety', 'devout', 'evangelise', 'catechise', 'holy', 'holiness' and 'preach' fit into this category, as does the very word 'religion' itself, along with 'religious' and 'religiosity'. A number of other words fall into this category only when used in a specifically religious context. Some such are 'save', 'redemption', 'salvation', 'worship', and 'adoration'. Of course, different categories of people are repelled in different ways. Some non-believers, for example, see these words as forming parts of the mumbo jumbo of superstition, while for many other people they merely represent a world that is inauthentic. Also to be found in this latter group are some people who believe in God but find religious jargon unattractive. All of this is unfortunate because it can impede the work of spreading the good news – the good news about the mystery that is God.

Reference has already been made to what the word 'religion' should perhaps mean. If it is understood as being concerned with re-establishing and maintaining contact with God, instead of being seen as merely a list of unwarranted rules and what appear, to many people, to be meaningless practices, it can regain its attractiveness. As for 'holy', much has been written about the original meanings of the Hebrew and Greek terms which we translate using that word. What is most important for our purposes, however, is to understand that the term 'holy', and its equivalents in other languages, came to mean 'of God' or 'dedicated to God'. Thus, in some of the New Testament writings, we find Christians being referred to as 'the holy ones' (or 'saints', although this word later took on a much more restricted meaning). This indicated that they had dedicated themselves to God – and thus were on the way to becoming fully human. For many in our time, however, the word 'holy', it seems, is hardly distinguishable from the hypocrisy which is associated with that other adjective 'sanctimonious', as is witnessed by the widespread use of expressions such as 'Holy Joe' and 'holier than thou'.

In short, the problem with these, and indeed all the words in the list – which, incidentally, is not intended to be exhaustive – is not the meaning they *ought* to have for us. Rather, it is the fact that bad religion has been widespread over a long period of time and has sullied a great many of the beautiful things that it has touched. Most tragically, it has portrayed an ugly, tyrannical, unloving god, or, more accurately, it has helped to bring about belief in the existence of innumerable gods fitting that description or, if not that description, something else with defects that are all too human. Small wonder that words associated with such gods have acquired the ability to repel. Unfortunately, a disliking for these words has encouraged not merely a rejection of gods which have defects that we commonly find in human beings, but has also discouraged openness to God.

Corrupting the message

The words 'evangelise' and 'evangelisation', which also appear in the above list of words that many find unattractive, stem from a Greek word meaning 'good news'. The good news in question is about our mysterious God. So how have we managed to make these words unattractive? It is, of course, possible that many of us associate them with attempts to preach down to people from a lofty, 'holier than thou' position. Another, not so easily identified problem, however, has been a centuries old tendency to cover what is inherently attractive with an excessively intellectualised veneer. This veneer is not insignificant. It is a substantial barrier. Distracted by it, we are in danger of not seeing or hearing the good news at all. Having noted that evangelisation, properly understood, is not primarily about adding to the knowledge that people have, or about mental assent to lists of beliefs, Donal O'Leary also points out that it is not something which comes at people from the outside. Instead, he sees the hearers of the good news becoming convinced about something that they already suspected before they received this communication. Their 'own hearts recognise, and delight in, and are transformed by, the authentic validity of such evangelisation' (O'Leary, p. 215). In situations in which 'heart speaks to heart', he says, it is not always necessary for the head to dominate:

> After nearly half a century trying to teach, preach, evangelize and catechize, I sometimes wonder whether we get lost, too easily, in the persistent search for rational clarity; whether we confuse religious knowledge (and religious behaviour) with a heart-felt sense of belonging to God; whether we lose sight of falling in love with God in pursuit of a more doctrinally explicit creed of beliefs. Is there a great danger of missing the stunning message of the Incarnation, and its implications for our humanity, through insisting too much on a prescribed progression through pre-arranged hoops and sequential stages of initiation? Evangelisation will always be grounded in the simplicity and profundity of the human heart.
>
> (O'Leary, p. 210)

The good news is inherently attractive. It is about love. In fact, a proper communication of the Gospel is a communication of love, and love is the only thing that can make sense of this mess in which we find ourselves. Love is what makes us whole, what completes us, what makes us truly human. At some level, it seems, we have intuitive awareness of this fact. That is why the Gospel can speak to us so clearly, provided we do not allow obstacles to get in the way.

At the time of Christ, it seems that bad religion, in the form of rules, observances, hypotheses and rationalisations which had the power to distract people from what was and still is important, became an obstacle for some people. Similar things can and do happen today. We often make the mistake of believing that Pharisaical behaviour belongs only to another time and another religion. There is, however, no reason to believe that it is any less widespread today than it was at any time in the past, although the rules and practices adhered to are clearly different. The worst aspect of Pharisaical religion and, indeed, all other kinds of bad religion is that they so easily become ends in themselves. Thus, they too become idols, or at least distractions, and thereby hinder reception of the good news about God. There is, however, no reason to despair. Jesus may well have used strong language in his communications with the Pharisees, but a Pharisee named Saul heard the good news one day when he was actually engaged in trying to fulfill what he saw to be his duties as a Pharisee. It is all a mystery to us, but it is also good news.

The mission of the Church is the mission of Christ. The Church exists to continue the work begun by Christ during his earthly mission. Its members have the job of spreading the good news of the kingdom, the good news about God. As St Paul says, the world was reconciled to God in Christ, and that message of reconciliation has been entrusted to us (2 Cor 5:19). As we have had reason to note, however, a great deal of extraneous matter has been added to the message over the centuries – different groups of Christians making different additions. One of the results of this process has been an obscuring of the essential message. Every now and then, some such extraneous items are removed – an example being teachings that God wishes us to punish people whose theology does not coincide with that of our denomination, whatever that denomination might be. Others, however, still remain, and they all have a tendency to divert our attention away from God. Strangely enough, because they tend to cause a certain amount of obfuscation, they might, at first sight, be thought of as part of the mystery. Instead, however, they hide the mystery. Indeed, they hide the very notion of mystery. They push us in wrong directions, away from mystery, and towards what is merely difficult to understand. The difficulty in understanding, moreover, sometimes results from the fact that what is being proposed is sheer nonsense – nonsense that is completely incompatible with the good news.

A common acceptance of such extraneous notions among most or all the adherents of a particular religion or denomination, or at least among most members of one sector of that religion or denomination, tends to indicate that those members share common misleading ideas about God. In fact, some of the extraneous ideas directly concern God. Now, clearly, in taking up this theme, we should discuss the truly monstrous ideas about God that have been in vogue at various times in Christian history. After all, it does seem to be the case that most of us, if not all of us, have some misleading ideas about God, and that those ideas are such that we could occasionally have in mind a god who is not God – even, sometimes, when we are praying. It may sound extreme to say that, at least some of the time, we worship a false god, but it does appear to be the case that something like that is fairly common. More specifically, we might say that we Christians vacillate between God, as revealed by Jesus Christ, and the god of our own or others' creation. In doing so, we are not unlike those Israelites described in the First Book of Kings by the prophet Elijah as wavering between two opinions, although there are significant differences. The Israelites concerned seem to have been hedging their bets by consciously keeping two lots of divinities in play at the same time, so to speak. Thus we find Elijah saying, 'If the Lord is God, follow him; but, if Baal, then follow him' (1 Kings 18:21). Christians who cling to their own misleading ideas about God seem to be rather different in that they are not usually aware of keeping two religions or, indeed, two gods in play at the same time. One of the reasons for this lack of awareness, perhaps, is the fact that there are highly influential people within the institutional churches who are among the ranks of the vacillators – vacillators leading the vacillators.

Almost Christianity and pseudo-Christianity

Over the centuries, Christianity has often been presented in various denominations as something that is rather like a club – albeit a very large one – with a complex list of rules and regulations, many of which have scant connection to the Gospel of Jesus Christ – and hence little, if anything, to do with God. Admittedly, although this tendency has led to bad things occurring, not everything that has resulted from such presentations has been of a wholly malign nature. Indeed, one would expect a lot of the adherents of this pseudo-Christianity to approach, and perhaps even match up to the high standards of the 'almost Christians' described by John Wesley in one of his most famous sermons. As he sees things, these almost Christians are honest, truthful, and loving. They give to the poor, clothe the naked and feed the hungry. In addition to all this, these people have a form of godliness, inasmuch as they do nothing that is forbidden in the gospels. They do not, for instance, seek revenge. Nor do they limit themselves to cheap and easy forms of kindness. They regularly set aside time for prayer, and their behaviour at the table of the Lord says only 'God, be merciful to me, a sinner'. These people, moreover, are sincere. They want to serve God, and have a heartfelt desire to do God's will. Is it possible, asks Wesley, to go as far as this and still be merely almost a Christian? Indeed it is, he says, and adds that he himself was almost a Christian for many years. Wesley goes on to say that three things are lacking in people who are almost Christian: faith, love of God, and love of neighbour. Only with these can a person become what he calls 'altogether a Christian' (Wesley, pp. 11–19). It may seem odd that Wesley should say neighbourly love is lacking in the people he describes as almost Christians when he has already described them as honest, truthful and loving. The meanings that we attribute to the word 'love', however, vary enormously, and it would seem that the love expressed by the almost Christian is of a different order to that which Wesley has in mind when he talks about the altogether Christian.

Love of this order will be discussed along with faith in the next chapter. For the moment, it is worth pausing to reflect a little longer on the fact that people seeking to know Christ have often been presented with a religion that urges them to be no more than *almost* Christian. It is also worth reflecting on the fact that this kind of religion has managed to survive for a very long time. One cause of the success that such pseudo-Christianity has had in spreading its message appears to have been the employment of threats of the wrath of God upon the disobedient by those in positions of authority. Indeed, control through fear seems to have been common enough in numerous churches for a very long period of time. Heaps refers to how, in his younger days, the authority figures he encountered in his own church used fear rather than love as a motivating force to keep people close to God. 'In many cases', he says, 'people seemed to respond, not from love, not from reason, but from fear. The fear has gone and so have they' (Heaps, p. 36). Heaps is referring to his experience within the Roman Catholic Church. We all know, however, that threats of fire, brimstone and various other horrors were used by preachers and teachers in numerous other denominations over long periods of time. It is well worth pointing out, of course, that, while all this was going on, authentic preaching of the good news was also taking place within at least some of those churches. We can be sure of that. We are never abandoned, but the fact remains that most of us are adept at placing obstacles in the way of the Gospel. One such obstacle is fear – fear, that is, of a god who is certainly not God. Even today, however, fear continues to be used as a controlling mechanism in some corners of Christianity.

Reference was made earlier to a widespread fear of change. It is not hard to see how unhealthy situations can be entrenched if fear of damnation through disobedience of authority figures is added to this more basic feeling of unease regarding change. In spite of this, we might expect some sort of change to come about when the abuse comes to an end, or, for one reason or another, loses some of its effectiveness. Even then, however, truly radical change is likely to be hampered. The basic fear of change to which we have just referred is likely to persist even if authoritarian use of fear as a control mechanism is no longer in play. Let us suppose, for instance, that when threats of divine wrath lost their impact or simply disappeared, many of the people referred to by Heaps not only rejected the version of Christianity to which they had formerly been affiliated, but went on to embrace atheism and replaced their former trust in God with trust in something else. Was this not a radical change? It certainly was, up to a point, but it was not as radical as many may be inclined to think it was. The fact is that, in practice, atheists and many of the people who describe themselves as believers appear to have a good deal in common. They either reject or pray to a god that does not exist – often, perhaps usually, a somewhat cruel and frightening monster. In other words, the same ogres that were around in the days of Heaps' youth are still in play. It is merely the roles they play in the lives of some people that have changed. Faith in such ogres is clearly not faith in God, and rejection of those same ogres does not amount to rejection of the mystery that is God.

The problem of fear as an obstacle to the spreading and reception of the good news rears its head in yet another form because of our tendency to take and apply quotations from the Bible literally and simplistically. There are numerous biblical references to fear of God. Now, de Mello, as we have seen, holds that we hate what we fear. Even if we substitute the word 'hate' with 'do not like', it seems that a serious problem arises if we fear God. De Mello recounts that, occasionally when talking to him, people say that fear of the Lord is the beginning of wisdom:

> But wait a minute. I hope they understand what they're saying, because we always hate what we fear. We always want to destroy and get rid of and avoid what we fear. When you fear somebody, you dislike that person. You dislike that person insofar as you fear that person. And you don't *see* that person either, because your emotion gets in the way.

> (de Mello, p. 117)

This said, the fact remains that fear of God is referred to in numerous places within the Bible as something to be encouraged. We are told in several books of the Old Testament, for instance, that fear of the Lord is the beginning, the origin, or the root of wisdom.

We are also told that those who fear the Lord are blessed (Ps 128:1–4). Both Jewish and Christian biblical scholars, however, tell us that, in such contexts, the Hebrew word which is usually translated as 'fear' is closer in meaning to 'awe', although neither 'awe' nor 'fear' entirely captures its meaning. Some scholars explain it as signifying a person's awareness of that which is totally overwhelming, as well as totally good and beautiful. We might say, then, that awareness of God as entirely awesome, totally good and the source of all beauty and love is the beginning of wisdom. Nevertheless, in spite of this more positive meaning that is given to the word usually translated as 'fear' in those Old Testament texts just mentioned, one might expect that, given the general thrust of Jesus' message, it would not appear at all in writings coming after his death and resurrection. Surely it would be replaced by 'love', or something of that ilk. The fact remains, however, that the theme of fear of the Lord is found in a small number of texts in the New Testament literature. It could, of course, be claimed that, in her Magnificat, Mary is merely quoting Psalm 103 when she says that God's faithful love extends from age to age to those who fear him (Lk 1:50), but, whatever we make of that, no similar explanation seems to be applicable to a text in Luke's other work. In the Acts of the Apostles we are told that the churches in Judaea, Galilee and Samaria walked in the fear of the Lord (Acts 9:31).[3]

Writing in the fourth century, St Hilary of Poitiers sees no contradiction between fear and love. Having pointed out that, in texts such as those referred to above, 'fear' is not to be understood in the sense it has in common usage, he goes on to say that, for us, fear of God is composed entirely of love (St Hilary, Ps 127:1–3). Not all of the commentators who emphasise the difference between fear of God and what we normally mean by fear agree entirely with this last point made by Hilary. However, we can surely say this: if it is the case that we can know God only through love, anything that is not in some way absorbed by or into love can only be a hindrance. That must be as true of fear (awe, wonder, a sense of what is overwhelming) as it is of anything else. After all, even faith that can move mountains achieves nothing of any value without love (1 Cor 13:2–3).

In short, then, love of God should certainly entail or be accompanied by wonder, admiration and an awareness of being overwhelmed, in a positive sense, by the divine. When love is replaced by terror, foreboding, horror, trepidation, or fear that makes us cringe, as has clearly been the case from time to time in numerous sections of Christianity, a false god is proposed, and the religious institution concerned promotes only itself. Promotion of such fear may serve to protect institutions, but it can hardly be described as a servant of the good news. As St John says: 'There is no fear in love, but perfect love casts out fear; for fear has to do with punishment, and whoever fears has not reached perfection in love' (1 Jn 4:18). His reference to punishment here makes it clear that he is talking about the kind of fear that is likely to cause us to cringe, run, hide, dread, or simply give up.

CHAPTER FOUR

Faith, Love and
the Mysterious God

Clearly, it would seem that, if we are to move on, we must have faith in the mystery that is God. But what is faith? As Albert Nolan observes, theologians can be tempted into imagining that, with divine revelation, they have privileged knowledge of the mystery that is God. Often, he acknowledges, it is said that this is faith rather than knowledge. However, 'in practice theologians and believers generally treat revelation as a kind of knowledge that can be pitted against scientific knowledge'. Faith, he goes on to say, is often wrongly thought of as a privileged kind of knowledge about a collection of dogmas, doctrines, and moral principles. It should rather be viewed as a kind of commitment: 'It means choosing to take the mystery seriously. In the face of transcendent mystery we can just walk away and ignore it or we can commit ourselves to it. We can choose to trust the mystery, to put our faith in it' (Nolan, pp. 36–8).

Earlier, I mentioned the fact that much of what is usually presented as religion is little more than a collection of hypotheses, conjectures and contentions, along with rules about practices to be performed by adherents. Often the hypotheses, conjectures and contentions – and sometimes even the obligatory practices – are spoken of as 'the faith', and they thus come to be regarded as essential. Speaking as a Roman Catholic bishop, Geoffrey Robinson says that some matters are indeed essential, but he finds in the history of the Church a tendency to go beyond those essentials. 'In reading again some of the history of the fourth and fifth centuries,' he says, 'I have found myself constantly asking, "How could mere human beings claim such certainty concerning the inner life of God or the exact manner in which Jesus was both human and divine?"' Should there not come a point, quite early in such speculation about the divine, he asks, 'at which we should bow before the mystery of God rather than attempt to spell it out in poor human words?' (Robinson, pp. 237–8).

It seems then that, even among Christians, faith in God is often discussed solely in terms of believing a certain number of claims as facts, including some of the conjectures about God to which Robinson refers. This can lead to strange attitudes and reactions. One fairly common reaction when challenges are made to such conjectures, for instance, appears to be fear of losing one's faith. Thus we find that, when doubts are expressed by others, some people react by resorting to statements such as: 'I do not wish to discuss these matters'; 'I want to keep to a simple faith'; and 'you are putting my faith at risk'. What they refer to as their 'faith', of course, is not usually simple. In some cases, the list of claims that are said to constitute the faith which they claim as their own is quite long, and what links the various elements is far from obvious – if, indeed, there is anything that links *all* the elements. Even before they encounter the doubts of others concerning one or more of these matters, people such as those under discussion may well have developed doubts of their own. In fact, the fear I have just mentioned is, I suspect, always associated to doubts which these so-called believers have. They do not want to confront those doubts because they have been led to believe that their faith is largely, if not exclusively, about accepting certain teachings. They are thus reluctant to join in conversations provoked by the doubts of others because they fear that, if they listen to the arguments of these others, they will put their faith in danger. They have been told that they must give intellectual assent to certain teachings, but they have doubts about at least some of those teachings. Given such a state of affairs, any well-founded arguments against those teachings which are presented to them by other people are likely to make intellectual assent on their part difficult. In fact, the whole situation is odd because well-founded arguments could conceivably make intellectual assent downright impossible. It is easy to understand, then, why some people might feel that exposing themselves to challenging arguments could endanger what they have been told is their faith. We surely have to face up to the craziness of this state of affairs. As Simone Weil says, 'Intellectual adherence is never *owed* to anything whatsoever. For it is never in any degree a voluntary thing' (Weil, p. 60. Emphasis mine). It is not difficult to see how observations such as this could lead some people to think that faith is nonsense. However, those who see Christian faith as consisting essentially in giving intellectual assent to lists of claimed facts and the performance of certain actions are labelling as 'faith' something that is quite different to its namesake in the gospels. As we shall see, moreover, they are also usually asserting that God is not really all that much of a mystery after all.

It is sometimes said that this problem of seeing Christian faith as merely intellectual assent to a list of claims arises as a result of confusing faith with belief. There seems to be some truth in this, but it has to be said that much depends upon the meanings we attribute to the words 'belief' and 'believe', and, of course, to the word 'faith'. Suppose, for instance, you say that you believe Canada is a larger country, in geographic dimensions, than Brazil. Your statement about the relative sizes of the two countries concerns belief about facts, and has a relationship to *knowledge* of facts – the belief being either well founded or mistaken. Such use of the words 'belief' and 'believe' does not capture or encapsulate what is meant in the New Testament writings by faith. The terms 'belief' and 'believe', however, are also used in a very different way. Suppose, for instance, you are taking part in a conversation about the suitability of a certain young man for something or other, and you declare: 'I believe in him'. The meaning of the word 'believe' here clearly differs considerably from the meaning it has in the above statement about Canada and Brazil. It also differs from the meaning it has when atheists say that they do not believe in God. When you say that you believe in the young man, you are not saying that you believe in the fact of his existence ('I believe he exists'). You are saying rather that you trust him, that you consider him to be worthy of your trust. In this sense, belief *is* close, and, if applied to God, is identical to the biblical notion of faith. If we turn to the New Testament, we find that the Greek words which are usually translated as 'faith' or 'to have faith in' are *'pistis'* and *'pistein'*. These words can also be translated as 'trust' or 'trust in'. Thus we read in some translations of the fourth gospel: 'Trust in God; trust also in me' (Jn 14:1).[4] We could just as well translate this passage as 'Believe in God; believe also in me' or 'Have faith in God and have faith in me'. The meaning in all three cases would be the same. Even outside of religious contexts, we use the word 'faith' in a somewhat similar way. In the case of the young man mentioned above, for instance, instead of saying that you believe in him, you could say that you have faith in him, meaning that you trust him, or that you trust him to get on with it, whatever 'it' may be, or perhaps even that you trust him to become something wonderful. Returning specifically to Christian faith, then, we can say it is about abandoning ourselves, in total trust, to God.

Serious problems can arise as a result of the fact that, in religious circles, faith is often associated with the word 'belief' only in the sense of believing facts or lists of claimed facts. The obvious and very real danger is that we come to see faith as consisting only in believing certain hypotheses or conjectures about God, even certain definitions. Some statements about God, for instance, 'God is love' or 'God is the Supreme Being', may seem unproblematic, but it is often the case that religions, or rather some of the people who take on leading roles in religions, claim much more detailed knowledge about the divine. As we have already noted several times, what we have to bear in mind is the fact that God is mystery. It is simply not possible for God to be grasped within a concept or even within a series of concepts. Robinson's comments quoted above, however, point to a tendency among Christians to either forget the notion of mystery altogether or else play mere lip service to it.

Saying all this in no way amounts to denying entirely the importance of belief about facts where faith is concerned. Trust in someone involves or presupposes certain such beliefs about that person. Within the context of Christian faith, we could take as an example belief that Jesus really was a person who lived on our planet. Robinson says that if someone does not believe this, then such a person can hardly be called a member of the Christian Church. This is one of those beliefs that he regards as essential. It seems, however, that, all too often in religions, belief in lists of claimed facts that human beings simply cannot know takes over. It becomes the main issue, and sometimes, it seems, the only issue.

The history of debate about the Trinity provides an example from within the ranks of Christianity of how we can thus become sidetracked from what is important. For many centuries, a major point of contention between two large sectors in the Church has concerned the Holy Spirit. One group claims that the Spirit proceeds from the Father and the Son, while the other claims that the Spirit proceeds from the Father through the Son. Does anybody really know what he or she is talking about at this level of theological debate? Can we really speak authoritatively about the inner life of God? In practice, of course, my use of the words 'group' and 'sectors', when referring to two sectors in the Church, should be modified. Whatever may be the positions taken up by the *leaders* of the churches concerned in this dispute, it is far from clear that all, or even most members of the two groups consciously make such claims. Indeed, on one occasion when I discussed the matter with a group of Christians, they told me that they had been totally unaware of the controversy until I mentioned it to them and that they had never really considered the meaning of that particular part of the Creed. Those people could well be, and, I imagine, are representative of a large percentage of both groups. Perhaps, at some level, most Christians intuitively recognise the fact that definitions of matters which belong to the realm of mystery are necessarily defective, limited and limiting.

Definitions spring from the world of analysis, investigation and working things out. They dwell, we might say, in the world of the intellect. It could, however, be argued at this point that there are statements, declarations, teachings, or whatever we want to call them, which come from, or are related to, what Jesus revealed. Is the intellect not necessarily involved in grasping what is conveyed in such teachings? Simone Weil discussed this very point in a letter she wrote to a priest in 1942:

> The dogmas of faith are not things to be affirmed. They are things to be regarded from a distance, with attention, respect and love. They are like the bronze serpent whose virtue is such that whoever looks upon it shall live. This attentive and loving gaze, by a shock on the rebound, causes a source of light to flash in the soul which illuminates all aspects of human life on this earth. Dogmas lose this virtue as soon as they are affirmed.
>
> (Weil, p. 48)

The bronze serpent to which she refers is, of course, the one made by Moses during the period when the Israelites were in the desert. If anybody who had been bitten by a snake looked upon it, he or she would live (Num 21:4–9). In St John's gospel, Jesus makes reference to it, saying: 'And just as Moses lifted up the serpent in the wilderness, so must the Son of Man be lifted up, that whoever believes in him may have eternal life' (Jn 3:14–15). The word translated here as 'believes' is again a form of the Greek verb *pistein*, which was mentioned above. Those who have faith in Jesus, those who trust him and commit themselves to him, will have eternal life. This is not a mere affirmation. It is not something that can be fully grasped by the intellect, and, when we reduce it to that level, those wonderful effects to which Weil refers cannot result from it. She continues, saying that, 'The propositions "Jesus is God" or "The consecrated bread and wine are the body and blood of Christ", enunciated as facts, have strictly speaking no meaning whatsoever'. This should not be understood as a denial of either doctrine. She goes on to explain by stating that the value of propositions such as those just cited 'is totally different from the truth contained in the correct enunciation of a fact'. An example she gives of such correct enunciation of a fact is: 'Salazar is head of the Portuguese Government', which, of course, he was at the time of writing. 'Paris is the capital city of France' might be a more suitable example in our time. The value of propositions concerning matters of faith, she goes on to say, 'does not strictly speaking belong to the order of truth, but to a higher order; for it is a value impossible for the intelligence to grasp, except indirectly, through the effects produced. And truth, in the strict sense, belongs to the domain of the intelligence' (Weil, pp. 48–9). In response to this, some people might feel the need to point out that Jesus is the Truth (Jn 14:6). Weil, however, is not denying this. She is merely indicating what we might call the demarcation lines between the domain of intelligence and that which is inaccessible to mere intelligence. She was herself no stranger to mystical experience, and was thus aware that there is a kind of understanding which is beyond under-standing – understanding that is beyond the limits of our purely intellectual capacities. If we try to reduce the sphere of faith to facts that can be understood by our intellects we will end up with something that is neither of faith nor of any value for the intellect.

If we allow God to be God in our lives, however, we will be transported far beyond the pettiness, and, indeed at times, downright silliness of our earthly quarrels about lists of things to be believed as factual. Faith, as we have seen, is about trust and commitment. In its deepest meaning, it concerns our relationship with God, and God is mystery. If we take this on board, Nolan's words quoted earlier, take on a new poignancy: '[Faith] means choosing to take the mystery seriously. In the face of transcendent mystery we can just walk away and ignore it or we can commit ourselves to it. We can choose to trust the mystery, to put our faith in it.' But, if faith is principally about a relationship, what is to be said about revelation? We can say, it would seem, that some facts about God are revealed: God is love; God loves us; God forgives us; God saves; and so on, although, as we shall have reason to note a little later, we should be more than a little wary of thinking that we really can understand fully what is meant by 'God is love', or, indeed, any other statements about God that we see as being revealed. Principally, however, what we call divine revelation is revelation *of* God, although some information *about* God comes along with that revelation. In other words, it is more about knowing God than knowing lots of facts about God.

In his prophecy of the new covenant – which is also quoted in the Letter to the Hebrews – the prophet Jeremiah writes of a time when it will no longer be necessary for anyone to teach his or her neighbours and relatives that they should learn to know God. Instead, he says, speaking on behalf of God, 'they shall all know me' (Jer 31:34). This statement is made in the context of a prophecy that God will plant his law in the hearts of his people. The law, of course, was of enormous importance to the Israelites. Observing the law was discussed by them in terms of walking in the way (or ways) of the Lord. There is at least a hint of intimacy, therefore, in a statement that God's law will be placed in the hearts of the people. The Hebrew word for 'heart' was used to designate the very centre of a person, not merely the centre of some of his or her emotions. The theme of intimacy becomes even more intense, moreover, in the book of Jeremiah's contemporary, Ezekiel, where it is stated that God's breath or spirit will be placed in the hearts of people, and will cause them to walk in God's laws (Ezek 36:27). This reference to walking again evokes the notion of the way – the way of the Lord.

As we move on to the New Testament writings, moreover, it becomes clear to us that the way of the Lord is something that transcends the mere observance of laws. When St Paul finds that some of the Corinthians are being distracted from what is important, he tells them that he is going to show them a way that far exceeds anything else they have ever known or encountered. This is the way of love, and what follows this statement is his famous hymn of love. Without love, he tells them, nothing has any value (1 Cor 12:31–13:13). 'Let all that you do be done in love,' he says, later in the same letter (1 Cor 16:14). Love, then, is the way, and, when Paul was writing these words, the movement that later came to be called Christianity was also known as the Way. Earlier in his life, Paul (or Saul, as he was known in those days) had been on the road to Damascus with the intention of arresting members of the Way and taking them back to Jerusalem. As is well known, he had some sort of mystical experience during this journey. Luke tells us that he heard a voice saying: 'I am Jesus whom you are persecuting' (Acts 9:5). With that statement, Jesus clearly identified himself with the Way, but he was not merely giving his backing to a movement. Jesus *is* the Way (Jn 14:6). Jesus, if you like, is the law, and we can participate in that law. We can walk in the Way, because we have the Holy Spirit. Paul himself both echoes and clarifies Ezekiel, saying: 'God's love has been poured into our hearts through the Holy Spirit that has been given to us' (Rom 5:5).

St John refers to the same thing in a different way. 'God,' he says, 'is love, and those who abide in love abide in God, and God abides in them' (1 Jn 4:16). Thus we see that the author of *The Cloud of Unknowing* was very clearly in line with a major biblical theme when he wrote that we can come to God only through love. In and through love we can know another human being, and we can even know God. Those who love, St John tells us, are born of God and know God (1 Jn 4:7). Having said this, however, even here we need to beware of forgetting the warning that the author of *The Cloud of Unknowing* gives about expecting too much from our intellects. Any attempt to fully, or in any sense adequately, capture the *meaning* of love within a mere concept is doomed to failure. Love itself is in the realm of mystery, and not surprisingly so, since God is love. Through our own experience, we can have some kind of inkling of what love is, but we cannot fit it into a concept and give an adequate description of it in words. There may be some who are inclined to dispute this. The word 'love', after all, is used to designate an emotion of fondness or warmth toward a person or persons, and most of us have felt some sort of affection for another person. The same word, moreover, is also used to indicate feelings of sexual attraction, and, again, most human beings who have lived beyond childhood have experienced such feelings. In other words, it might seem that love is not all that much of a mystery to us after all. When the word 'love' is applied to God, however, we move into a sphere that transcends all of this, and when St Paul urges us to do everything in love, he too is speaking of the transcendent because he is talking about our acting under the influence of the Holy Spirit, who is love. When the author of *The Cloud of Unknowing* says that we can come to God only through love, he is surely talking about our acting (loving) under the influence of, indeed, through the power of, the Holy Spirit. Saying all this, of course, by no means amounts to saying that human affections are incapable of being transformed through the action of the Spirit. In speaking of such transformation, however, we are taking our discussion again into the realm of the mysterious.

It become obvious, after a discussion like the one we have just had, that faith and love have to be considered together. Faith in God without love is nonsense. Any discussion of either has to be a discussion of a relationship. Faith, in its richest meaning, is complete and loving abandonment and commitment to God. Such a relationship, of course, involves God and a human person. As such, we now need to say something about the human person.

CHAPTER FIVE

Knowing God and Knowing Me

It is sometimes said that the way we think about God has a profound effect upon the way we think about ourselves. But is this really the case? It seems to me that our thoughts about God are likely to have some effect upon our self-image. While acknowledging this, however, we should be wary of the temptation to exaggerate. The faulty notions we have of and about ourselves do not always mirror well what we think of God. Although, for instance, any person's self-image is likely to be pretty monstrous, it is not likely to be as bad as that same person's image of God. Some readers may immediately be inclined to disagree, saying it is surely the case that most believers have always thought of God as infinitely better than they are. On one level, I would have to accept that this is probably true of all Christians who are of sound mind, and, one imagines, of most other people who believe in God. If, however, we go back to our discussion of the influence of faulty religion and to what was said about the petty, petulant, needy and jealous god of religion referred to by Rohr, we may find some inconsistencies in the way we think about God. While believing that God is infinitely better than they are, many people also manage to have beliefs of an entirely opposing nature. Not only are most of us less petty, petulant, needy, jealous and unforgiving than the god that we envisage at least some of the time, but we are also *aware*, at some level or other, that this is the case. When nagging feelings of discomfort arise within us about an apparent lack of good qualities in God (that is, in our conception of God), we desperately search for justifications. We make excuses for God.

Although we say we believe that God is infinitely better than we are, in practice, much of what we read, hear and think about God just does not back up this claimed conviction. Undoubtedly, a number of texts from the Old Testament have contributed to the problem. Even among the writings of the Old Covenant, however, there are more than a few hints that God is love. The oft-quoted Psalm 23 is an obvious example: 'Even though I walk through the darkest valley, I fear no evil; for you are with me; your rod and your staff – they comfort me … you anoint my head with oil; my cup overflows … Surely goodness and mercy shall follow me all the days of my life' (Ps 23:4–6).

In a similar vein, Deutero-Isaiah writes: 'Can a woman forget her nursing-child, or show no compassion for the child of her womb? Even these may forget, yet I will not forget you' (Isa 49:15). What matters most, of course, is Jesus' message about God's love and forgiveness, which is illustrated so clearly in the parable of the prodigal son (Lk 15:11–32) and the illustration of the lost sheep that is joyfully carried home by the shepherd (Lk 15:4–7). Strangely, however, many Christians have often preferred to latch on to parts of the Old Testament scriptures in which God appears to be portrayed by the authors as rather violent and, in short, not very nice. And yet, many of those same Christians, one imagines, have experienced no impulse to imitate these supposed characteristics of God. At least in some ways, the notions they have about how they are and how they should be are not as bad as the ideas they have about God.

The fact remains that, whatever the influence of how we see God upon how we see ourselves, our self image can be – and perhaps in most cases is – enormously problematic. We have noted more than once that the problems we have in thinking about God seem to stem largely from our reticence or refusal to take seriously the fact that God is mystery. A similar problem arises when we fail to take seriously the mystery that is each of us. In his discussion of mystery, Albert Nolan sees the word being used in two ways. One refers to that which is beyond the limits of our intellect. In other words, it refers to what is unknown and also unknowable. The other is illustrated in the expression 'murder mystery'. We may not know who committed the murder, but this is not something that is, by definition, unknowable. Nolan is inclined to refer to this latter kind of mystery as a puzzle. Puzzles, in theory, can be solved (Nolan, p. 31). When we turn to discussion of God and ourselves, however, we find that we are most definitely in the realm of mystery. Here we come up against what, in this life, is not merely unknown, but unknowable. Even if we fail to appreciate the fact that we too are mystery, surely all of us are at least puzzled from time to time by our own behaviour, our own reactions to things, our own attitudes, and, above all, our own ignorance about ourselves. This ignorance is highlighted in a device called the Johari Window, which is used in the world of psychology to improve, among other things, self-awareness. Its inventors were Joseph Luft and Harry Ingham, the word 'Johari' being a combination of their first names. The central tool is a diagram of a window with four panes or sections.

What everybody knows about me.	What only I know about me.
What other people know about me, but I do not.	What nobody knows about me.

The window represents an individual person – although it can also be used to represent a group of people. One of the four panes represents what is common knowledge about the person – at least within a particular group. A second represents hidden knowledge about this same person. He or she has this knowledge, but nobody else has access to it. A third represents knowledge about the person which others have but which the person himself or herself does not, while the fourth pane represents knowledge about this person which nobody has.

In practice, things are likely to be somewhat more complex than we may at first imagine. Words like 'knowledge' and 'awareness' are not always accurate descriptions of what is actually possessed.

We sometimes deceive ourselves. Other people, moreover, sometimes manage to convince us that a certain description of us is true when it is not. Some of what has been taught to many Christians about the concept of humility has probably added a good deal to this kind of confusion over many years. It is often said that humility is truth, but the way in which it is often presented seems to lead instead to a pack of lies concerning both negative and positive aspects about oneself. Having been taught to put themselves down 'in all humility', it seems that some people do precisely that when talking to other people, even when the knowledge they have about themselves in regard to the qualities under discussion is much more positive. Such tension and denial is unnecessary, unhelpful and unhealthy. In some cases, moreover, people may eventually succeed in convincing themselves as well as others about such untruths.

Teresa of Avila's *Interior Castle*, on the other hand, paints a picture of something that is in stark contrast to any depiction of ourselves as worthless trash, although she makes it abundantly clear that she is well aware of the damage inflicted on us by sin. Teresa speaks of the human soul (perhaps we might prefer to say 'the human person') in terms of a castle made from a single diamond or a transparent crystal. The soul of a just person, she goes on to say, is a paradise in which God delights. With such a statement, it is clear that we have moved away from a vision of ugliness and worthlessness to one of amazing beauty and value. As we have already noted, Teresa is in no way inclined to downplay the part played by sin in our lives. Nor, however, is she inclined to downplay the role of God or the loveliness of God's creation. We may well be wretches, but we are lovely wretches, and, of course, we are loved. With such an acknowledgement, moreover, we have also been transported from the realm of the merely puzzling into the realm of mystery, although it could be said that even the Johari Window hints at mystery, if it is taken seriously. Teresa sees nothing as being capable of comparison with the exquisite beauty and abilities of a human soul. What's more, no matter how sharp our intellects may be, we are no more capable of comprehending the beauty and abilities of a human soul than we are of comprehending God (Teresa of Avila, ch. 1).

Above we noted the difference between knowing things about God and knowing God. In regard to self-knowledge, the situation is somewhat different. Although, in this world, we will never have full understanding of what we are and who we are, we can acquire a fair amount of knowledge about ourselves and, indeed, about other people. As is the case with God, however, it is also essential that we come to know ourselves. Teresa takes up this theme. She says that the castle (the soul) has many rooms, and that God lives in the principal chamber. There, it is possible for God and the soul to converse. She then goes on to talk about the need to enter one's own castle. This, of course, is the same as talking about entering into oneself. Teresa acknowledges that this can seem incongruous. It is, she says, rather like asking someone to go into a room in which he or she is already standing. This said, however, Teresa points out that there are various ways of being in a castle, and some people settle for living in the courtyard, in the area where, in the case of a real castle, sentries might be found. Such people, she says, are unaware of all those rooms inside and of who it is that lives in that delightful place (Teresa of Avila, ch. 1).

The elephant in the room

We shall return to the theme of knowing oneself shortly. Before that, however, we need to acknowledge the elephant in the room. In short, all this talk of beauty and delight could be confusing to people who are inclined to wonder how sin fits into things. A simple response might be that there is likely to be plenty of it in and around the courtyard to which Teresa refers. Having said this, however, it is worth sounding a note of caution. When many Christians talk about sin, they manage to switch off the listening abilities of those they are addressing. Indeed, a criticism that one occasionally hears directed at most of the various Christian denominations is that they appear to be obsessed with sin – especially sexual sin. Thus we find Christianity being described by some people as a discouraging religion. If that is the impression given, something has gone seriously wrong in the process of spreading the good news, which has clearly been perceived by many as bad news. The fact is that being labelled as sinners is not necessarily such a bad thing. In several of the New Testament texts in which the word 'sinner' (or 'sinners') is used, reference is also made to Jesus' keeping company with people who are labelled as such. In a number of cases, moreover, some people complain about the kind of company Jesus keeps. These critics, it seems, do not regard themselves as sinners, and, therefore, have not yet begun walking on the right path (or way). Take, for example, the account of a woman with a bad reputation anointing Jesus' feet when he was in the house of a Pharisee, or the account of his visit to the house of Zacchaeus, a reformed tax collector. On both occasions, others were astonished that Jesus should be content to be in the company of such people. St Matthew, however, tells us that, on one occasion, Jesus told the chief priests and elders of the people that tax collectors and prostitutes were getting into the kingdom of God before them. In spite of hearing what John the Baptist had to say, these authority figures had not repented, whereas the prostitutes and tax collectors had done just that (Mt 21:28–32). The continuing problem was not the easily identifiable sins of these two groups, but the self-righteousness of the chief priests and elders. At least at this point in their lives, there was no turning around for them, no new beginning, but for those others who were regarded as public sinners the situation was very different.

The discovery and acceptance of one's sinful status is actually an occasion for rejoicing. Spirituality begins at that point. On another occasion recorded in Luke's gospel, Jesus remarks that, upon hearing John the Baptist, the tax collectors had acknowledged God's justice, whereas the lawyers and Pharisees had refused to be baptised, and had thus rejected God's plan for them (Lk 7:29–32). In short, the discovery and acceptance of one's sinful status is a necessary step, and should be a wholly positive experience. Spirituality really does begin at that point, if the person concerned recognises his or her complete dependence upon God and trusts God totally.

Faith and the kingdom

This brings us to the subject of God's kingdom: 'The time is fulfilled, and the kingdom of God has come near; repent, and believe in the good news' (Mk 1:15).[5] If it is understood as meaning merely 'to feel remorse about something', the word 'repent' is not a suitable translation of the original Greek word used by the evangelist in this text. That word, *metanoeite*, does indeed indicate remorse, but it also indicates a turning around of the person, a conversion. If we confine ourselves to 'remorse' as a translation, we are in danger of attributing too much importance to feelings of guilt, feelings of inadequacy, and even feelings of inferiority. Guilt does indeed serve a purpose, but wallowing in it can be very destructive. Likewise, feeling inadequate or inferior to other people is very negative and, on the whole, unproductive. As Julian of Norwich puts it: 'for just as by God's courtesy he forgets our sin from the time that we repent, just so does he wish us to forget our sins and all our depression and all our doubtful fears'. Rather, she says, we should trust in God's love (Julian of Norwich, p. 168).[6] When true conversion takes place, the people concerned certainly experience the sadness of remorse. At the same time, however, they become joyfully aware of the solution. God really does love them and forgive them. A complete turnaround is possible and, what is more, it is happening now.

It is happening because the kingdom of God is here. The Greek word translated as 'kingdom' is *basileia*, and kingdom is indeed what it normally means. It is probable, moreover, that Jesus chose that word or its Aramaic equivalent[7] because many Jews at that time tended to talk about God and the anticipated messiah in terms of kings and rulers.[8] Given our very different circumstances, however, the English word 'kingdom' does not readily indicate what is involved in Jesus' pronouncement, notwithstanding the fact that it has been the most widely used translation within Christian circles for many centuries. 'Kingship of God' or 'the reign of God' would seem to convey better what Jesus appears to have intended. This is because what is under discussion is the possibility of God taking over – God being in control, if you like – and of our consenting to that takeover. There has been a rupture in the relationship between God and humanity, but that is not how things should be. Without God being in control, without God being the very ground of our being, we are seriously unwell. As we have already noted, this state of being unwell is exhibited, among other things, in our tendency to try to make God fit into our own petty vision of things – our tendency to try to control God, rather than let God take control. Salvation is all about being reattached – or, perhaps rather, being properly connected – to the source of life and love, to the source of our full humanity, so that we can be fully human and fully alive, so that you can be fully you and I can be fully me. We could even talk about being immersed in God – mystery immersed in mystery. Salvation comes with the kingdom (or, if we prefer, with God's reign), with God taking over. All this talk about salvation being concerned with proper attachment to the source of life, indeed to life itself, may seem to be reminiscent of what Lactantius and St Augustine said about the origin of the word 'religion' (or *religio*), to which I referred earlier. True Christianity, the Way, if you like, has to be about such establishment or re-establishment of connections because it is about salvation, about the kingdom that is here now. As we have had reason to note, however, the kind of religion that people often encounter, including much that is called Christian religion, does not match up to this ideal.

Knowing ourselves
But what does all this have to do with the need for us to know ourselves? And what does our need to know ourselves have to do with our need to know God? The fact is that our tendency to invent our own versions of God is matched by a tendency to make up versions of ourselves. In fact, our behaviour in this regard can be quite complex and bizarre. It is often said that, in a metaphorical sense, we all wear masks, but it is not simply the case that each of us has only one mask. A person can have different masks or personas which he or she puts on for different people that he or she meets and for different sets of circumstances. One mask could

be worn by a particular man, for instance, when he tries to sell computers in the shop where he works. This he might see as an appropriate persona for him in his role as a salesman. Another, which he sees, rightly or wrongly, as impressive, he might wear when trying to gain the attention of a young woman whom he would like to be his girlfriend. A third appears on the scene when he speaks to his overbearing father or mother. With this mask he appears subservient while hiding any unhappiness he may have in that role. This tendency towards what is inauthentic begins early in our lives as we learn and acquire coping strategies. As children, we learn to behave in certain ways and to feign certain attitudes in order to please other people, to prevent their being angry with us, or to manipulate them into pleasing us. This process, it seems, continues as we get older. There are probably many other reasons in this broken world why we create false images of ourselves. I shall make no attempt to list them. Whatever our reasons may be, what is important to note here is the fact that we do create and portray these false images, these masks, if you prefer. Moreover, these works of fiction do not merely prevent others from meeting the real you or the real me; they make it very difficult indeed for me to meet the real me and for you to meet the real you. It is important to note at this point, however, that this process is not the cause of the fact that we are mystery. In fact, it seriously impedes our ability to appreciate the mystery.

Bearing all this in mind, it is easy to see how Teresa of Avila could say that some people live in the courtyards of their personal castles. Although such people may be well aware of various aspects of their bodily appearance, they know practically nothing about their inner being. They need to be introduced to their castles. In other words, strange though it may seem, they need to be introduced to themselves. Prior to that introduction, what they know is a work of fiction, a monster, if you like – perhaps even a series of monsters. Teresa, we have seen, refers to God living in the central chamber of the castle (the soul). This coincides, of course, with the biblical notion of the Holy Spirit living in the heart or centre of the person. Clearly then, the inauthentic images of ourselves have to die, and our inauthentic lives have to be lost, so that we can find that central chamber where we will find not only ourselves, but the kingdom of God too.

At the beginning of this chapter we discussed the notion that our image of God affects how we think of ourselves. It is sometimes also stated that, notwithstanding what we read in the Book of Genesis about our being created in the image of God, most, perhaps all, of us have a tendency to create God in our own image. What we encountered in the first two chapters of this present book, however, appears to indicate that this claim fails to take account of just how complex the process of producing false gods can be. In the light of what we have just discussed, moreover, it could also be added that, without considerable modification, this claim betrays excessive optimism about our ability to know who we are. In reality, we tend to experience great difficulty in this regard. Any so-called 'images' of ourselves that we may manage to produce are in danger of being nothing like our authentic selves. In response to this observation, the claim that we create God in our own image could be modified. It might instead be suggested that the image of God which each of us has is a reflection of how we see ourselves rather than an image of what and who we really are. The claim then would be that we create God in the image of our inauthentic selves. As noted above, however, given the input of bad religion into the lives of many people, even this claim is likely to need modification. The gods that we invent are often much worse, it seems to me, than the false selves that we invent. What really matters, however, is the fact that, if we do succeed in being introduced to our real selves, we will find God. There is an intimate connection between the discovery of self and the discovery of God.

The importance of relationships

Relationships are among the best aids in the search for self. It is not difficult to see how close encounters with other people could lead us to become aware of some of the falseness that we have been portraying to them and indeed to ourselves. In practice, however, a deepening of such relationships can take us far beyond such awakening. In truly intimate relationships, some of that falseness simply disappears. Some of the masking melts away. This said, it is worth noting that not all of the relationships that people call friendships achieve this level of closeness. This we know is true even of many marriages. Where real intimacy is achieved, however, the assurance of loving and being loved causes masks to fall or melt away. Perhaps not all of them disappear, but any amount of progress leads to a revelation of some truth about the people involved in the relationship. Relationships with other people, however, are not the only aids available to us in the search for self. In her *Interior Castle*, Teresa discusses another route. Her book, of course, is about one's relationship with oneself and one's relationship with God through prayer. Now, because of the effects of faulty religion, some of us may have difficulty in seeing that human relationships and prayer have much in common. A little reflection on St John's Gospel, however, may help us to alter that. Jesus says to those gathered at the Last Supper: 'I have called you friends' (Jn 15:15), having already said: 'This is my commandment, that you love one another as I have loved you' (Jn 15:12). Prayer is all about relationship with God. In relating to other people, moreover, we can be in prayer, just as we can be when we set aside a few minutes to be alone with God in a church, in a park, in a prison cell, in a garden, or in a desert. Coming to know yourself in the way described by Teresa and coming to know other people and yourself in relationships are also ways of becoming aware of God, of coming to know God. We get to know God in getting to know ourselves and other people. But perhaps we should say a little more about prayer.

Prayer

An enormous amount has been written on the subject of prayer, but some presentations are very complex and, for that very reason, can be quite discouraging. One of the virtues of *The Cloud of Unknowing*, on the other hand, is its simplicity. The author of that work, however, appears not to be enthusiastic about its having an enormous circulation. Indeed, he recommends it only to people who are seriously committed followers of Christ, not merely in their active lives, but also at the highest levels of the contemplative life that may be attained in this earthly existence. Mention of the contemplative life is not surprising, given that what is discussed in the book is contemplation, the meaning or aim of which is referred to right at the beginning of the text: 'Here begins a book of contemplation called *The Cloud of Unknowing*, in which a soul is made one with God'. It may seem odd to begin a discussion of prayer with *The Cloud of Unknowing*, or indeed with any discussion whatsoever about contemplation. Introductory works on prayer are, one supposes, usually expected to begin elsewhere. The present book, however, is principally concerned with God as mystery, and it is what the *Cloud*'s anonymous author has to say on this subject that is of particular interest to us here, as well as what he has to say about matters linked to the mystery, including our attitude to it. Strange though it may seem it is in some ways easier to talk about contemplation than it is to discuss other forms of prayer because contemplation is simple – not always easy to achieve, perhaps, but certainly simple. After our discussion of it, we shall consider what can be gleaned from that discussion and then applied to other forms of prayer. There may be differences among the processes involved (as we shall see), but there are also similarities in all forms of prayer.

Although he refers to the 'work of contemplation' and the need to 'labour at it', the author of *The Cloud of Unknowing* also makes it clear that contemplation is not a product of our intellectual labours, and warns against the danger of our deceiving ourselves in this regard. Rather, he says, 'for the love of God take care in this work, and do not struggle in your intellect or imagination in any way. For I tell you truly, it cannot be achieved by that kind of struggle; so give it up and do not attempt it' (*The Cloud of Unknowing*, p. 26). Given this, the author's constant references to the *work* that the contemplative has to do could seem odd. In the passage just quoted, for instance, the reader is warned to 'take care in this work'. The fact is, however, that work of a kind does have to be undertaken by the would-be contemplative. In fact, the anonymous author tells us that those who habitually practice contemplation will find it is very laborious indeed, unless they have been practising it for a long time or have received special grace. There is, however, no contradiction in what he says here because the needed labour to which he refers consists in the setting up and maintenance of what he calls a cloud of forgetting. Having become aware of the cloud of unknowing that is above us, and is thus between us and God, he says, we need also to put a cloud of forgetting beneath us, so to speak. By this he means that, during periods of contemplation, we need to forget, or at least put out of our minds, 'everything that was ever created'. Every act, attribute, thing or person should be hidden under this cloud of forgetting. He admits that some of what is put out of our minds in this way is good. Where contemplation is concerned, the author tells us, nothing but God should be in one's mind. Indeed, he goes on to say that even thoughts of God's own kindness and of Christ's passion are of little or no benefit here. At this level of prayer, even thoughts of God's attributes can be a distraction. God alone suffices. Although it may be good at times to think about God's kindness, it is not part of the work of contemplation, and so it should be covered by the cloud of forgetting. He clearly understands that anybody attempting this will probably come up against problems. In the early stages, and even later, it is not likely to be easy to keep everything covered by this cloud of forgetting. As an aid, he suggests that his reader might want to make use of a word like 'God' or 'love', which can act as a shield against distractions (*Cloud*, pp. 26–9, 51).

> With this word you are to hammer down every kind of thought beneath the cloud of forgetting; so if any thought forces itself on you to ask what you would have, answer it with no more than this one word. And if, in its great learning, it offers to expound that word and tell you its attributes, say that you wish to have it quite whole, and not analysed or explained.
>
> (*Cloud*, p. 29)

The Cloud's author is well aware that one's first attempt at this work is likely to result only in the finding of darkness, but he says one should not give up:

> And so prepare to remain in this darkness as long as you can, always begging for him you love; for if you are ever to feel or see him, so far as is possible in this life, it must always be in this cloud and this darkness. And if you are willing to labour eagerly as I tell you, I trust in his mercy that you will reach your goal.
>
> (*Cloud*, p. 22)

All this, of course, as we have already noted, is about contemplation. Now, contemplation consists simply in being in the presence of God. During his time as curè (parish priest) in a small town in France called Ars, Jean Vianney asked a certain man what he said when he prayed before the tabernacle in the church. The man informed the curè that he said nothing. 'I look at him,' he said, 'and he looks at me.' Some of those who achieve this most simple of all kinds of prayer can remain in such a state for long periods. It is easy to see that it might not be possible for everyone to achieve such prayer. It is also easy to see how the advice given in *The Cloud* about the need to become aware of a cloud of unknowing and to work to bring about a cloud of forgetting can apply to anyone attempting it. What is to be said, however, about those who have not reached these levels of prayer? In spite of what he says about the book being suitable only for contemplatives, the anonymous author of *The Cloud* does make some mention of other people, although, even then, he seems to have in mind only people who are *aiming* at contemplation. He accepts that anyone, male or female, who nurtures hopes of achieving contemplation will first need to meditate on some of those very things that he tells contemplatives to put below the cloud of forgetting. Indeed people hoping to reach the contemplative state without having first meditated many times on such matters as Christ's passion, their own sinfulness and the goodness and kindness of God will, he says, certainly fail (*Cloud*, p. 29). In saying this, he is not alone.

Other spiritual guides speak of stages in prayer – stages that people pass through on the way to the higher levels of contemplation. Of course, even the author of *The Cloud of Unknowing*, along with other long accepted authorities on prayer, can provide only guidelines. After all, we are talking about God, and God does not have to take us through any particular stages in any particular order. The Holy Spirit blows where the Holy Spirit wills. Accepting that the general guidelines have some value, however, what can we say about people who, in spite of years of praying, do not pass through all those stages? Teresa, who has long been widely regarded as an authority on contemplative prayer, discusses this kind of problem in her *Way of Perfection*. According to her own testimony, however, for fourteen years she was unable to even practice meditation without reading. She supposes that, not only will many other people have similar experiences to her own, but also that some others will be unable to meditate even with the aid of reading, these last mentioned being able to pray only vocally. She goes on to say, moreover, that the minds of some people are so active that they are incapable of dwelling on one thing. They are so restless that, 'if they want to pause to think of God, a thousand absurdities, scruples, and doubts come to mind'. She clearly sees it as important to be aware, moreover, that not everybody is called to contemplation, and, she says, being a contemplative is not necessary for salvation; it is a gift (Teresa of Avila, p. 99). This last point echoes a comment made in *The Cloud of Unknowing* that contemplation is the easiest work of all when the person concerned is helped by grace, 'but otherwise it is hard, and you can do it only by miracle' (*Cloud*, p. 22).

So where does what we have said thus far leave all those people who are not contemplatives? Where does it leave people who, if Teresa of Avila is right, can only pray vocally? As far as the aims of this book are concerned, it leaves them in much the same place as contemplatives. Prayer of any kind is about the development of a relationship. It is about knowing God, and everything we have said about the importance of distinguishing between knowing God and knowing things about God applies to all of us. If contemplative prayer is one's gift, so be it, but even if it is not, one should still be aware that any description, definition, or concept of God that one conjures up in one's intellect (or is provided by the intellects of other people) is certain to be totally inadequate. Whatever the nature of our prayer, and whatever the nature of our call in life, we need simply to trust in the mystery that is God. If, with God's help, we commit ourselves to the mystery, the mysterious God will take care of everything else.

St Paul famously says that the Holy Spirit helps us in our weakness. When we do not know how to pray, the Spirit intercedes on our behalf with sighs (or groans) that are unutterable – too deep for words to express what they convey (Rom 8:26). In practice, it seems to me, we never know how to pray. If we are given to vocal prayer, it might be appropriate on occasions to say something like 'I don't know what to say'. In the end, whatever our style of prayer may be, we just have to let God take over. That is what the kingdom is about. St Paul tells the Romans that the Holy Spirit enables us to cry out '*Abba*, Father'. The Spirit bears witness along with our spirit that we are children of God (Rom 8:15–16). Paul's use of the Aramaic word *Abba* here is significant. He does not merely say that we cry 'Father'. His intention is clearly to show how we are joined to Jesus, who used the word *Abba* when addressing his Father. He uses the same device in his letter to the Galatians, who, it seems, were being persuaded by some other people that the law was necessary for salvation. God, Paul tells us, has sent the Spirit into our hearts, and the Spirit cries, '*Abba*, Father' (Gal 4:6).

One occasionally hears discussion about whether or not the word *Abba* would be more accurately translated by 'dad' or 'daddy' on the grounds that (at least in the English speaking world) these are the words most commonly used by people when addressing their fathers. These words, it is argued, reflect better the intimacy of Jesus' relationship with his Father. In practice, of course, some of the people who make use of the word 'dad' do not even like their fathers, and some of those who address their male parent as 'Father' have a very deep affection for him. All of this, however, is beside the main point. It is the Aramaic word that is significant simply because it is the word that Jesus used. In his translation of it into Greek, Paul appears to have made no attempt to indicate anything other than 'father'. His intention, it seems clear, was to emphasise the Christian's relationship with Jesus. With Jesus, we cry *Abba* (the word that he used), and when we do not know what to say, the Spirit cries *Abba* for us. The word indicates everything that is the mysterious relationship into which we need to enter.

Needless to say, no image of an earthly father (or mother) will suffice to represent God to us. In fact, there could be problems attached to such imaging for people whose fathers are not at all fatherly. Something extremely important that we need to note in the gospels and in Paul's writings, however, is Jesus' total trust in *Abba*. Our faith, our trust, includes trust in Jesus, trust in the fact that he is our brother, that he has taken us to himself, and that we, along with him, can put all our trust in *Abba*. This is all very mysterious, of course, but the fact is that, regardless of what words we use, God remains mystery, and mystery is where we can be ourselves.

CHAPTER SIX

Poverty and Mystery

The connection between poverty and mystery may not be immediately obvious to everyone. One reason for this is undoubtedly the fact that the centrality of poverty to Christianity has often been very well hidden. Moreover, the tension that exists between the two ways in which the word is used in Christian tradition has probably added to the confusion. We need to begin our discussion, therefore, by looking at the places that those two meanings occupy within our tradition. This will necessitate abandoning explicit mention of mystery for a few pages, but we shall return soon enough. The first and most obvious meaning of the word 'poverty' is decidedly unpleasant. It denotes deprivation, and deprivation is at times so bad that it results in the lack of a suitable place of shelter, inadequate clothing, starvation and death. The second meaning of 'poverty' signifies a virtue. We shall first address deprivation.

Poverty as deprivation in scripture

There is a good deal about poverty as deprivation in the Bible. Long before the birth of Jesus there had been a long and well-rooted tradition among the Israelites about caring for widows, strangers, the poor and other vulnerable people. Those who planted crops, for example, were told that they should not harvest all of them. They should instead leave some around the edges of their fields for poor and needy people. Similarly, people who had orchards were instructed to leave some fruit on their trees for the same purpose (Lev 19:9, 23:22; Deut 24:19). There was also legislation about jubilee years (Lev 25:8–55), when land that had been sold in the immediately preceding period of fifty years (since the last jubilee year) was to be returned to its original owner, and debts were to be suspended or perhaps even wiped out. We know little about the degree to which such legislation was obeyed. Some scholars have pointed to the problems that would have been attached to making it work in its entirety. It is important, however, that we see the symbolic value of such laws. At the base of Israelite thinking on these matters was the conviction that the world belongs to God alone. Thus we read: 'Land will not be sold in perpetuity, for the land is mine; with me you are but aliens and tenants' (Lev 25:23). We also read: 'The earth is the Lord's and all that is in it, the world, and those who live in it' (Ps 24:1); and, of course: 'every wild animal of the forest is mine, the cattle on a thousand hills. I know all the birds of the air, and all that moves in the field is mine' (Ps. 50:10–11). Given this ideology, Timothy Gorringe tells us, 'there can be no absolute rights to private property. All human beings are no more than God's tenants, and in the use of their property have to conform themselves to God's standards' (Gorringe, p. 116). According to those standards, there must be no poor people among the Israelites (Deut 15:4). In this light, it is easy to understand what lies behind the legislation referred to above, especially perhaps the rules about not harvesting all the crops and fruit.

At the time of Jesus there were, in fact, many poor people, but he continued the tradition of promoting justice to those in need, and took it up to a new level or dimension by identifying himself with the poor and other people who were (and are) disadvantaged in one way or another (Mt 25:35–46). The seriousness with which the early Christians treated this teaching, moreover, is reflected in the Acts of the Apostles: 'There was not a needy person among them, for as many as owned lands or houses sold them and brought the proceeds of what was sold. They laid it at the apostles' feet, and it was distributed to each as any had need' (Acts 4:34–5).

The Church Fathers

The title 'Fathers of the Church' has long been applied to a number of influential Christian teachers and writers who lived between the first and eighth centuries after Christ. Lactantius, St Augustine, and St Hilary, to whom we have already referred, were among them. A number of these men expressed very strong opinions about the problems attached to the accumulation of riches. St Ambrose, for instance, tells us that when we give a part of what we possess to poor people, we are merely handing over to them what is theirs. Although the world has been given to all of us, and not just to the rich, there are people who have taken some of these common possessions for themselves (St Ambrose, ch. 12, n. 53). Ambrose was a westerner who lived in the fourth century, and wrote in Latin.

Over in the east, and writing in a similar vein at much the same time, but in Greek, was John Chrysostom. He declared that, if we do not share our wealth with poor people, we are guilty of stealing from the poor and depriving them of their means of life. It is their wealth as well as ours (Chrysostom, ch. 6). Similar comments were made by others among the ranks of the Church Fathers. It might seem, therefore, that they all advocated the abolition of private ownership. That may, indeed, have been an ideal in the minds of many of them. At least some, however, considered the problems that might arise if nobody owned anything. One such was Clement of Alexandria. He refers to Jesus' call for us to feed the hungry, give drink to the thirsty, clothe the naked and give shelter to the homeless. How could we do this, he asks, if we all divested ourselves of the things needed to supply such aid? Riches which can benefit others are not to be thrown away, he says (Clement of Alexandria, p. xiii–xiv). This, however, in no way detracts from the above statements by Ambrose and John Chrysostom. We should be prepared to share what we have. Ultimately, what we own is common.

Thomas Aquinas

Much later, in the thirteenth century, Thomas Aquinas addressed the question of whether or not we can justify the private ownership of things. When we read what he has to say, it seems obvious that, in his deliberations about private property, he takes into account the fact of our brokenness, the fact that we have a tendency to get things wrong a fair amount of the time. He gives three reasons for justifying the private possession of things. The first is that we are all more careful to procure what is for ourselves than we are to acquire what is for everybody. Secondly, there is more order when each of us is responsible for looking after something specific than when we all have to look after the same things. Finally, people tend to squabble more often when there is no division of possessions. There is greater peace when we are all content with what is ours. This said, however, Aquinas goes on to talk about the use of the things that we own, saying that we should be ready to let others have them when they need them. In other words, we should possess things as common, and not as ours (Aquinas, q. 66, art. 2). Aquinas adds strength to this last point in a later section where he deals with the question of whether or not a person who is in desperate need and takes what is the property of another is guilty of theft. In cases of emergency, he says, when there is urgency (when, for example, someone is in imminent danger, and no other possible remedy is available), one may take what is needed from among the possessions of another person, and it may be taken either openly or secretly. Properly speaking, says Thomas, such an act is neither theft nor robbery (Aquinas, q. 66, art. 7).

It is obviously the case that, if time and circumstances allow, we should ask for help rather than just take another's property. Thomas does not in any way encourage us to steal. Stealing, however, is to be understood as taking the property of another person *against the reasonable will of that person*. Clearly, love demands that we try our best not to cause any kind of unnecessary upset to other people, and, usually, the taking of property without permission causes a great deal of upset – even, on occasion, a sense of personal violation. The exception in extreme circumstances which is mentioned by Aquinas, however, serves to remind us of the fact that creation is for all of us. It is wrong to steal, but it is also wrong not to give. We do not have exclusive rights to the things we own. As some people put it, we are stewards of the things we possess.

Of course, all of this was written a long time ago. Since then, various philosophers, including John Locke, have had their say about the justification of private property. In the twentieth century, moreover, the communist experiment erupted and failed, and capitalism continued to develop into the complicated, and difficult to understand thing that it is today. As a result of these developments, and innovations in the world of technology and elsewhere, our situation in regard to money and possessions is very different to that which prevailed in the days of the Church Fathers, or in the days of Aquinas. Nevertheless, influenced by these, we may still feel that what we have left over after we have satisfied our needs should be given to the poor. For most people in the richer countries nowadays, however, financial arrangements are quite complex. In trying to work out what is left over after they have satisfied their own needs, they need to set aside various sums which may not yet have been paid but will be collected at some future date: money for rent or mortgage payments; insurance of various kinds; telephone bills; heating and lighting bills; income tax claims; various bills for their children; pension contributions; money for the replacement of motor vehicles, computers, furniture and so on. The basic teachings of the Church Fathers and Aquinas, however, are still applicable. What is important for us to note is the fact that those men were aware of a tendency we all have: the tendency to forget at times that the creation is for all of us.

In more recent times, numerous writers from various churches have reminded us of these teachings, but they seem to have received scant attention. John Paul II, for instance, refers to what he, along with a number of other recent popes, calls a right to private property. However, he says, 'Christian tradition has never upheld this right as absolute and untouchable. On the contrary, it has always understood this right within the broader context of the right common to all to use the goods of the whole of creation: *the right to private property is subordinated to the right to common use,* to the fact that goods are meant for everyone' (John Paul II, 14. Emphasis his).

Of course, being a good steward means having a sense of responsibility. Responsible people will thus take knowledge of hygiene into account and advise, for example, exclusive use of toothbrushes. For obvious reasons, we should also advise exclusive use of certain items encountered in the sphere of medicine. A sense of responsibility leads us to see that giving to those who need money or certain things is not the same as giving to those who merely want such things. Bearing that in mind, we see that we should not, for instance, spoil our children. When applied to children, the words 'spoil' and 'ruin' seem to lose a lot of their impact for some people, who seem to see such spoiling as simply giving special treats. The fact is, however, that excessive pampering really can cause damage. It can cause a weakening of character. I am not, of course, advocating anything less than good care of children. In dealing with them, parents and others should be nothing less than generous. Spoiling children, however, makes it difficult for them to grow into people who share what they have, and those who are unaccustomed to sharing find it hard to embrace poverty in the second sense, which we shall discuss shortly.

As for the first meaning of poverty, we have touched on at least some of what makes it central to Christianity. More central to our purposes in this book, however, is the fact that Christ's identification with the poor touches on mystery because we cannot hope to fully understand what is involved in it. What, however, is to be said about the second meaning?

Poverty as virtue
We can say immediately that, when we turn to a discussion of poverty as virtue, we find ourselves dealing with something that seems to be essential for anyone wishing to take the mystery of God seriously. All the evangelists tell us that Jesus spoke on many occasions about the dangers attached to riches and about the need for poverty among his followers. We gather from these teachings that one of the principal problems attached to money and possessions is their tendency to impede our relationship with God.

Indeed, at times, they even take up a place in our affections and aspirations that should be reserved to God. Already, we might think, this aspect of Jesus' teaching is quite different, and in some ways quite separate from what we discussed under the heading of poverty as deprivation. There is, however, a connection to the notion of ownership as stewardship. Good stewards have a healthy detachment from the things in their care. They do not seek all their security in them. They do not put all their hope in them. They are not enslaved by them. If they allowed any of these things to happen, they would not be good stewards. It is their very detachment that enables them to make the goods in their care available for other people. If, on the other hand, we become so attached to our possessions that we are unwilling to share them with others who are in need, we become slaves to our possessions. We need them too much. They have a hold on us. In a sense, we might say, it is not so much a matter of us owning them, rather that they own us. If we allow God to be replaced by money or possessions in this way, we cut ourselves off from the source of life and love. It is hardly surprising then, that this kind of worship of a false god leads to injustice. The simple fact is that we cannot serve both God and money (Mt 6:24; Lk 16:13). Where our treasure is, there will our hearts be also (Mt 6:19–21; Lk 12:34). The story of the rich young man who went away sad when Jesus advised him to sell what he had and give it to the poor seems only to emphasise that fact (Mt 19:16–22; Mk 10:17–22; Lk 18:18–23). In short, it is harder for a rich person to get into the kingdom of God than it is for a camel to get through the eye of a needle (Mt 19:23–6; Mk 10:23–7; Lk 18:24–7).

Mention of the kingdom brings to mind the first of the beatitudes. There are, in fact, two lists of beatitudes, one appearing in Matthew's account of the Sermon on the Mount, and the other in Luke's gospel. Matthew's list of beatitudes is longer than Luke's, and the latter is followed by a list of woes, which are not recorded by Matthew. There are also significant differences in wording. Luke, for instance, refers simply to those who are poor being blessed, whereas Matthew talks about the poor in spirit. In both cases, however, it is the first beatitude that concerns the poor, and, in both cases, reference is made to the kingdom. In Luke's gospel, Jesus tells the poor that the kingdom of God is theirs (Lk 6:20), and, in Matthew's account, the poor in spirit are told that the kingdom of heaven is theirs (Mt 5:3).[9] Most of the other categories of people mentioned in the two lists of beatitudes are told of some *future* benefit that will accrue to them. Those who mourn, for instance, will receive comfort, while peacemakers will be called children of God. In both lists, however, the present tense is used for the poor (or the poor in spirit). The kingdom *is* theirs. This kingdom, we have seen, is the reign of God. God takes over, and we put all our trust in God. There is so much that we do not understand, but we trust, we have faith, in the mystery. For that to happen, however, we have to latch on to the first beatitude. It seems, then, that there is most definitely a connection between poverty and mystery. Without poverty, we are simply not open to the mystery of the kingdom.

But which kind of poverty and which version of the beatitude should we take up – Matthew's or Luke's? On several occasions I have been a witness to discussions among members of religious orders about the meaning to be attributed to their vow of poverty. The opinions expressed have always been far from uniform. Generally speaking, the disagreement tends to centre on the apparent conflict between two positions: one that seems to be influenced by Luke's first beatitude and another that seems to take its inspiration from Matthew. In my experience of such conversations, one group has taken the view that the poverty of those who take the vow should be material, while the other has held that the important thing is to have an attitude of detachment from possessions, such an attitude being referred to as poverty of spirit. Given what we have said so far, it is, of course, easy to see that attachment to any possessions we may have can be problematic. However, it is not really enough merely to be able to say 'I could live without this or that'. We can reach much deeper levels. A first step is to face reality and accept the fact that most of us are in possession of numerous things, either in the sense that we do actually own them, or that we have exclusive or very easy access to them. A second is to reflect on the two aspects of poverty of spirit identified by the famous Russian Orthodox Archbishop Anthony Bloom. The first aspect, he says, is the discovery that we are not masters of anything that is in our possession. In that sense, we can say that we do *not* possess anything. The second aspect – and this could, no doubt, seem paradoxical to some of Bloom's readers – is in the realisation that we are rich because God has made us rich. Everything we have is gift, a gift of God's love. This love, Bloom goes on to say, 'is manifested continuously and fully' when we see and accept that, in reality, we *possess* nothing. As soon as we claim something as ours, as soon as we become possessors, love is lost.

The kingdom, says Bloom, is 'the sense that we are free from possession, and this freedom establishes us in a relationship where everything is love – human love and love divine' (Bloom, pp. 14–15). In short, it seems to me, the meanings of words like 'possess', 'own' and 'have' vary with the degree of our realisation that everything is gift, and with the attitude which springs from this realisation. Bearing this in mind, we can see how it is possible to talk about having the various riches of life, including one's talents, and even about being in possession of material things, while being poor in spirit.

But does this mean that material poverty has no importance in the context of poverty as virtue? Jesus' comment about rich people, camels and the eye of a needle certainly seems to indicate that some sort of material poverty is important in some way. And, indeed, it is not difficult to see why this may be the case. It is far from easy to be poor in spirit when one is steeped in material wealth. That said, there are people who do own a great deal and yet seem not to be attached to what they own, not to be enslaved by their possessions or distracted by them from what is important. The fact that this could be the case was, of course, specifically referred to by Jesus when he added to his declaration about camels and eyes of needles that nothing is impossible to God. The fact remains, however, that money and possessions have powerful distracting abilities. This is not merely the case when we are immensely wealthy. Even if we have very few possessions but covet the excessive wealth of others, we are clearly not poor in spirit.

But saying all this does not suffice to deal with all eventualities. Whatever problems we may have concerning attachment to possessions can be exacerbated by tendencies toward self-delusion. We can easily fool ourselves into believing that we are poor in spirit. All we need in order to achieve this state of affairs, it seems, is a little obfuscation here and a little rationalisation there. Thus we may convince ourselves that we need certain expensive luxuries for our work, for our sanity, or perhaps simply because we have few other pleasures in life.

A particularly interesting form of rationalisation is found among the ranks of those who own very little or even, at least in theory, nothing at all, but, in spite of this, live in the lap of luxury. Such situations can exist for a variety of reasons. There are people, for instance, who are very well cared for by far wealthier friends or relatives, while others are members of very rich organisations. Ironically, even people who have taken a vow of poverty in certain religious orders can be found in this latter group. The money given to the order or reaped from investments can be well used for apostolic activities and to provide food and the other simple necessities of life for the members. A little rationalisation, however, would suffice to extend the meaning of 'necessities of life' con-siderably. This, no doubt, is one of the causes of those animated discussions among people with vows of poverty about the meaning of the poverty that they have vowed. I have certainly encountered members of such orders for whom material poverty is a very important aspect of their following of Christ.

When I was eighteen years of age, a Franciscan friar gave up a fair amount of his time to teach me Latin, a subject I had not learned at school. The knowledge I acquired in this way proved to be quite useful some years later when I decided to become a theologian. More significantly, however, this same Franciscan was the first person to awaken in me any awareness at all of the virtue of poverty, although, admittedly, the process he started was (and still is) a pretty slow one.

Since that time, I have encountered numerous other members of religious orders whose simple way of life has been an inspir-ation. Some years ago, for example, I met a Dominican friar whose cell was entirely furnished with items that other people had literally thrown away. I have also encountered communities of religious sisters who lead very simple lives, relying on God's providence for the bare necessities of life while working hard for the sick and the poor.

The fact remains, however, that, in the situations in which some members of religious orders (often referred to simply as 'religious') find themselves, it is very easy for them to grow accustomed to the material advantages of what we might call a higher-middle-class lifestyle. Some of these religious, like some of those people who are lavishly cared for by rich friends or relatives, might claim to own little or nothing. That, however, changes nothing about the fact that they are accustomed to a way of life which gives a feeling of security about the material aspects of life and which is very comfortable indeed. Even if they acknowledge that this is a fair description of the state in which they find themselves, some of them may still claim that they are not attached to the luxuries they use and consume. It is certainly possible that this is the case, as we have already noted in regard to some exceedingly rich people. In both cases, however, there is clearly a danger of becoming attached at some future date to always having luxuries on tap. Exclusive, or simply assured use of something can be just as problematic as actual ownership of that thing, and so, of course, can growing accustomed to the acceptance of excessive generosity from friends, relatives, or anybody else.

In short, it is possible for us to have poverty of spirit even when we find ourselves in situations of great privilege, but we need to beware of rationalisations through which we try to convince ourselves that we have this virtue when we do not. The major issue, not just for members of religious orders, but for all of us, may well be poverty of spirit, but having many things, or simply having access to many things, can lead us away from that virtue.

This said, it is worth noting that no degree of even voluntarily embraced material poverty will suffice to guarantee the presence of poverty of spirit. Indeed, Clement of Alexandria highlights some of the dangers open to those who renounce possessions, such as that of becoming arrogant, pretentious, and contemptuous towards the rest of humanity, as if the renunciation were a superhuman achievement. Another is that of continuing to be consumed with desire for what one has renounced and regretting what one has done (Clement of Alexandria, xii).

Hiding the idols

In the second chapter, I said that money is easily identifiable as an idol. That would seem to be true, but it also seems to be the case that most of us are adept at fooling ourselves into thinking we are somehow immune to any danger of falling into the trap of treating money and other possessions as false gods, or even as major distractions. The problem was compounded at certain points in the history of Christianity, moreover, by a tendency in some of the churches to dilute a number of Jesus' teachings. It was widely taught over a long period of time, for instance, that much of what Jesus said about poverty was intended only for people who were described as seekers of perfection – monks, nuns, friars and religious sisters being among the more obvious examples of what was meant. In recent times, there has been a movement away from this kind of thinking on the all too obvious grounds that there is only one Gospel, and that this Gospel does not have two tiers. In other words, Jesus did not found or propose a Church with two divisions – one for first-class Christians, and another for those who are less committed. There is one Gospel for all. All Christians should, in some way or other, embrace poverty. However, some lasting damage was done by that corruption of the Gospel message, and the fundamental importance of poverty within Christ's teaching is still often downplayed.

At this point, it seems worthwhile to mention another easily identifiable idol which was mentioned in the first chapter of this book but which may not strike most people as something that is relevant to our present theme of poverty and mystery. That idol is power, and it is certainly something that we possess in various ways and in varying quantities. Clearly, it is not merely our own experience that warns us about the danger of both power and money. We have already noted Jesus' warnings about riches. As for power, he reminds the apostles that Gentile rulers lord it over their subjects. It is not to be so among his followers (Mt 20:24–8; Mk 10:41–5; Lk 22:24–7). In practice, however, like money, worldly power has played a significant role, and, indeed, as an invited guest, in large sections of the Church over very long periods of time.

When debate about problems of this kind takes place, there usually seems to be a temptation to confine things merely to a discussion of the behaviour of Church leaders. One of the reasons for this is probably a widespread tendency to refer to such people as 'the Church', as though all the other people, although referred to as members of the Church, are, in some way, not the Church. The fact is, however, that whatever our role may be in that Church, just as we all need to beware the danger of trying to serve two masters (God and money), so too do we all need to beware of having our heads turned by power. At a basic level, of course, power can be described merely as ability to do something. It is important, for example, to empower people by means of a good education. Clearly, power even in this basic sense of ability can be used in bad ways. Our main concern here, however, is power over other people. This kind of power can be particularly dangerous and particularly dehumanising. In addition to the damage it can cause to those over whom it is exercised, it can have a terribly corrupting effect upon those who wield it. It is, of course, commonly accepted that, when we do things together in groups, we need organisers and even sometimes individual decision-makers. These organisers and decision-makers have a certain amount of power with which they have been entrusted. We often call this kind of power 'authority'. Such authority, however, must never be exercised as anything other than service to others. Otherwise, it becomes a dangerous possession – an obstacle to poverty of spirit. It would be wonderful to be able to say that authority has always been exercised as service within the Church, but that has clearly not always been the case. All too often, like fear and money, abusive authority has been found where only love should reign.

While it is true that we should beware of the temptation to limit discussions of money, possessions and power to what some might call the power structures within the churches, the fact remains that Church leaders can be enormously influential. In most churches, the leaders tend also to be teachers. What they teach and how they behave in regard to such matters can influence the beliefs and behaviour of others. As was noted earlier, none of us develops his or her idols in isolation. Influential people within the religious groupings to which we adhere can play a major role in the development of such false gods when they allow other things to take up a position in the Church that only love should occupy. One assumes that none of us actually prays to money or power. In that sense, then, we can say that neither of the two is a false god. The fact remains, however, that they can impede openness to the kingdom. Worse still, they probably play major roles in the development of the gods to whom we actually do pray. Becoming free to know the mystery necessitates seeing these distractions for what they are.

Poverty and mystery

I began this chapter by saying that the connection between poverty and mystery may not be obvious to everyone. To see clearly how necessary poverty is if we are to succeed in being open to mystery, we need to reflect upon all the possessions we have that may be getting in the way. It should be easy enough for most of us to list such things as money and material possessions. The fact is, however, that we become attached so very easily to a good deal more than material possessions. We have already discussed the possibly corrupting and distracting effects of any power that we may possess. As for our talents, we are already well accustomed to calling them our gifts, but the meaning of that word can so easily be lost. One of the problems we tend to run into where talents are concerned is that of almost defining ourselves in terms of what we do rather than of what we are. And, of course, what we ourselves are is mystery.

Among the other possible attachments that we may have acquired during our lives are blind convictions about our countries, pet opinions about certain schools of thought or certain political parties, our own views of the world, and, perhaps most especially, our own ideas about God. We may not be accustomed to thinking of all these items as possessions, but the fact is that they are most certainly *ours*, and most of us, it seems, have a tendency to cling to at least some of them even more tenaciously than we cling to our material possessions. All these distractions, safety nets and comfort blankets have to be recognised for what they are, and we have to learn to put all our trust, not in them, but in our mysterious God. Once again, those words of Nolan come to mind. Faith, he says, 'means choosing to take the mystery seriously. In the face of transcendent mystery we can just walk away and ignore it or we can commit ourselves to it. We can choose to trust the mystery, to put our faith in it'. Properly understood, poverty of spirit is faith, and the only kind of faith that matters is faith in mystery.

CHAPTER SEVEN

Awakening to Mystery

One day, when he was in the centre of a shopping district in Louisville, Kentucky, Thomas Merton had an experience which could reasonably be described as both astounding and life changing. 'I was suddenly overwhelmed,' he tells us, 'with the realisation that I loved all those people, that they were mine and I theirs, that we could not be alien to one another even though we were total strangers.' Up to that point in time, Merton had seen his monastic life as involving separation from the world. In a flash, it seems, he saw this former way of looking at things as mistaken. He had awoken from what now seemed like 'a dream of separate-ness, of spurious self-isolation in a special world, the world of renunciation and supposed holiness' (Merton, p. 140). The experience did not cause Merton to question the reality of his monastic vocation. It was just the notion of separation from the world that he now saw as an illusion.

In his account of this experience, Merton does not make use of the word 'mystical'. In Christian circles, that term is normally employed to indicate something that has divine significance and that cannot be grasped by our normal intellectual capacities. Given the fact that Merton makes no use of the word in connection with this particular experience in Louisville, it might seem odd for a commentator on it to resort to such a description. What does spring to mind upon reading what he says, however, is that his insight seems to be closer to what we might call spiritual enlightenment than to intellectual breakthrough, by which I mean an insight that results, in some way or other, from some sort of reasoning process.

The difference between this latter kind and the kind of enlightenment that comes from the Holy Spirit and is beyond our control is of enormous importance. As Richard Rohr says:

> Enlightenment is precisely not like the layers of an onion. It's one great truth that you know in a moment. But you know it now and again when the false self gets out of the way. You don't work up to it. It's normally not cumulative. It's an epiphany. All of a sudden, walking from here to there you see it. You know it is given and not created. We can't hold on to it, but we must still return through daily prayer. Once we've known who we are in God, nothing less will satisfy us.
>
> (Rohr, p. 71)

Most of us, one imagines, have not had the kind of experience that Merton had in the shopping centre. Bearing this in mind, it seems likely that not everybody who reads about it will arrive at his conclusions. Using the same kind of reasoning processes as they have used on many other occasions, some people might argue, for instance, that separation from the world is precisely what *is* required of a monk. The way in which they would arrive at this conclusion, moreover, might well resemble, in some ways, peeling away, one by one, the layers of an onion. Just as the removal of each onion layer reveals another, progress toward the conclusion is made in steps or stages, each step depending for its appearance on the step that immediately precedes it. Reasoning in a similar way, on the other hand, other people might come to the conclusion that they agree with Merton. In other words, if we were to stay at this level of rational argument, peeling away at imaginary onions, we would easily see that there could be a good deal of room for disagreement among Merton's readers. So much would depend upon what each participant in the discussion meant by 'separation', and, of course, a great deal would also depend upon each one's vision of the world and of God. As for Merton, it seems that he was happy to go on living what was, in one sense at least, a somewhat separated life as a monk. His *attitude* to the rest of humanity, however, was no longer one of separation. He was aware of being one of 'them', or rather, he was aware, in a new way, that we are all 'us'. It seems not to have been the case, however, that Merton arrived at his new awareness as a result of any kind of reasoning process. It just happened. It follows then, that no amount of reasoned explanation by the present writer can be guaranteed to faithfully transmit Merton's insight. If, therefore, some people apply their reasoning faculties to what I have written, or even to Merton's own description of his experience, it matters little, on one level, whether these people claim to agree or to disagree with what he says. The simple fact is that, if they use only their intellects, people analysing the insights of someone who has received spiritual enlightenment are unlikely to fully appreciate what he or she is saying when expounding those insights. Merton's own insight seems to have come to him in a flash. It was, we might dare to suggest, an example of spiritual enlightenment.

In some cases, it seems, enlightenment such as this could be described as a grasp – at a level deeper than anything mere reasoning could ever achieve – of something that one already knew intellectually before the enlightenment occurred. The new grasp, however, is on a very different plane from that of the former intellectual understanding. This would seem to be a fair description of what happened to Merton in that shopping centre in Louisville. Surely it is safe to assume that what he suddenly grasped was not something that had no parallel, at some level, in what we might call his ordinary understanding. He, like many millions of other people, had read the gospels, and therefore knew about the Incarnation, the call for us to love one another as Christ loves us, and he also knew the universal nature of that call. He had an intellectual grasp of these things, and would, no doubt, have been able to give interesting and valuable explanations of them. After his Louisville experience, however, Merton knew that reasoned explanations are never enough. Thus we find him saying: 'I have the immense joy of being man, a member of a race in which God Himself became incarnate. As if the sorrows and stupidities of the human condition could overwhelm me, now that I realise what we all are. And if only everybody could realise this! *But it cannot be explained*. There is no way of telling people that they are all walking around shining like the sun' (Merton, p. 141. Emphasis mine). It seems that other people will grasp things in the way that Merton did only by means of enlightenment which comes from the Holy Spirit.

There are, of course, appropriate times and places for *thinking* about such matters as God, faith, and the Gospel, for using our reasoning powers to help us grapple with these deepest realities. Indeed, theology is often described as faith seeking understanding, and it does seem to have its usefulness. In spite of this, however, major problems are certain to arise when we place all our trust in our intellects, or those of others, and most of us, it seems, do have a tendency to fall into that trap – even those of us who are not inclined to describe ourselves as very intelligent. The simple truth is that the deepest kind of understanding available to human beings is neither accessed nor accessible by means of our reasoning processes. This truth is touched on by Merton himself:

> Then it was as if I suddenly saw the secret beauty of their hearts, the depths of their hearts where neither sin nor desire nor self-knowledge can reach, the core of their reality, the person that each one is in God's eyes. If only they could all see themselves as they really are. If only we could see each other that way all the time. There would be no more war, no more hatred, no more cruelty, no more greed … I suppose the big problem would be that we would fall down and worship each other. But this cannot be seen, only believed and 'understood' by a peculiar gift.
>
> (Merton, p. 142)

It is important to be aware then, that the kind of enlightenment to which Rohr refers, and which Merton appears to have experienced, is not a product of the intellect. It is pure gift, and it is beyond anything that can be achieved by the intellect alone. While spiritual enlightenment and intellectual breakthrough are to be distinguished, it seems to me that, through the power and activity of the Holy Spirit, enlightenment can come to a person when he or she is engaged in the very ordinary, intellectual process of reading what another has written. It can come also to someone who is listening to another person reading aloud from a book or an article. It is possible, for instance, that some people will experience something similar to Merton's own insight upon reading his account of what happened to him that day in Louisville. This can happen, one imagines (and perhaps always happens), when the reader is least expecting it. In such cases, we might say that spiritual enlightenment breaks through what would otherwise be a merely intellectual process. It was with this in mind that, when referring above to people using only their intellects to analyse the insights of a person who has received spiritual enlightenment, I merely said that they are *unlikely* to fully appreciate what he or she is saying. The Spirit blows where the Spirit wills. We are never really as successful at blocking the path of the Spirit as we may think we are. Given this state of affairs, we might hope that everyone would experience enlightenment upon reading any part of any of the New Testament writings, but we know well that we humans have an amazing ability to reduce even the birth, life, death and resurrection of Jesus to little more than an interesting and inspiring piece of history. Thus it becomes something to be dealt with on a purely intellectual level, with, perhaps, a touch of emotion thrown in here and there. This said, a sudden insight can come to any of us at any time.

Anthony Bloom tells us, for instance, that in the days of his youth he began looking for a meaning in life. One day, purely out of loyalty to the youth organisation to which he belonged, he attended a lecture by a priest, having been requested to do so by one of the youth leaders. He did not believe in God, and had first responded with violent indignation when the request to attend had been made to him. He had no wish to waste any of his time on such matters. As he listened, he tells us, 'I saw a vision of Christ and Christianity that was profoundly repulsive to me'. After the lecture, he hurried home to check the truth of what he had heard. He wanted to know if the gospels would give support to 'the monstrous impression' he had been given in the talk:

While I was reading the beginning of St Mark's Gospel, before I reached the third chapter, I suddenly became aware that on the other side of my desk there was a presence. And the certainty was so strong that it was Christ standing there that it has never left me. This was the real turning point. Because Christ was alive and I had been in his presence I could say with certainty that what the Gospel said about the crucifixion of the prophet of Galilee was true, and the centurion was right when he said, 'Truly he is the Son of God'. It was in the light of the Resurrection that I could read with certainty the story of the Gospel, knowing that everything was true in it because the impossible event of the Resurrection was to me more certain than any event of history. History I had to believe, the Resurrection I knew for a fact. I did not discover, as you see, the Gospel beginning with its first message of the Annunciation, and it did not unfold for me as a story which one can believe or disbelieve. It began as an event that left all problems of disbelief behind because it was a direct and personal experience.

(Bloom, xi–xii).

Another example, although this time involving a person who already believed in God, is very well known. One day, in the Porziuncula chapel, Francis of Assisi heard and suddenly understood the significance of Jesus' instruction to the twelve in St Matthew's gospel: 'Take no gold, nor silver, nor copper in your belts, no bag for your journey, nor two tunics, nor sandals, nor a staff.' The insight he had in this moment about the importance of what he came to call 'holy poverty' was life changing, not only for himself, but also for countless others who 'caught' the same insight on the rebound, so to speak.

Enlightenment comes from and remains within the sphere of mystery. It comes from the Holy Spirit, who is beyond the limits of our comprehension, and yet it brings us to a different kind of understanding – to the kind of understanding that Pseudo-Dionysius tells us is 'above vision and knowledge'. It may well be the case that enlightenment in the order of that experienced by Merton in Louisville is extremely rare. The fact is, however, as has already been stated several times in this book, that we all have to deal with mystery, in one way or another, whether we have experiences like Merton's or not.

It is, of course, common among Christians and many others to associate God and the notion of mystery quite readily with certain kinds of inexplicable events which they are inclined to classify as miraculous, and, indeed, some reported episodes of enlightenment have, on occasion, been described as such. Miracles are usually thought of and spoken about as events which lie beyond explanation by any of the sciences at a particular moment in time – the time, that is, when the event occurs. Most frequently, it seems, these events involve unexplained cures from illnesses or bodily deformities, and their occurrence usually causes some consternation among the witnesses and beneficiaries. Any tendency to think of mystery as being associated only with the realm of the spectacular or, at least, the unexplained, however, can lead us astray. An obvious problem with such a tendency is the fact that, as advances in scientific knowledge take place, at least some of the events that were previously classified as miracles will no longer be classified as such. Suddenly, scientists are able to explain certain happenings that they, and everybody else, had previously found puzzling. As a result, the cures in question (or whatever other events took place) now become part of what we consider to be ordinary. When this kind of thing happens, it is easy to see how some of the people who had previously been convinced that a miracle had taken place might now be disappointed. They had believed that the event concerned was a manifestation of the power of God, but now, it seems, it can be explained in other ways. The very existence of such disappointment gives rise to questions. Is God now thought not to have been involved in the event? Is God to be found only in the extraordinary, in the spectacular? Is mystery to be found only in events that seem to be incapable of having a scientific explanation?

I remember a conversation about miracles I had about thirty years ago with the American biblical scholar Roland Murphy. It seemed to him that such events as a baby being born, the sun coming up in the morning, a flower opening, and, indeed, any other events that speak to us of God could well be described as miracles. Surely he was right. In fact, surely everything that is not sin speaks to us of God. Everything speaks to us of the mystery that is God. The mystery, then, is in the ordinary as well as the extraordinary. Whether or not we are open to what is being communicated to us in the events that surround us and involve us is, of course, another matter, but the fact remains that mystery is most certainly in what we call the ordinary things of life. We ourselves are mystery, and we continue to be surrounded by mystery.

The fact that many of us appear not to notice this presence of mystery needs to be addressed. In an important sense, it seems we could truthfully say that both of the above-mentioned categories – what we tend to classify as ordinary and what we tend to classify as extraordinary – are, in reality, beyond the ordinary. In important ways, I would suggest, they are also beyond the experience of a good many of us – even, perhaps, the vast majority of us. It may seem strange to suggest that many of us have not experienced events which are so familiar to us that we call them ordinary. Is there not a contradiction there? If the suggestion were merely that, sometimes, some of us do not *really* experience *some* of the ordinary events of life, it would probably be viewed by most people as a good deal less controversial. After all, we are well accustomed to referring to the same problem in a slightly different way. We talk about people running away from reality some of the time. Excessive use of certain drugs, including alcohol, seems to provide more than ample witness to that. In recent years we have become accustomed to the warnings of those who see a danger of some people becoming content to live most of their waking hours in a so-called virtual reality provided via the internet. In addition to all this, many people have expressed concern about what they see as a flight from reality in the so-called cult of celebrity. The problem to which I am referring, however, appears to affect many more of us than are contained within the categories just listed. Indeed, in some spiritual writings it seems to be suggested that, although we may not be aware of fleeing reality, most of us, in a sense, sleepwalk our way through life, and this, it seems, may well be the case even for most of those people who are not only teetotal, but have also never used the internet and have no interest at all in what famous people get up to. De Mello is one writer who does not pull any punches when he addresses this issue:

> Spirituality means waking up. Most people, even though they don't know it, are asleep. They're born asleep, they live asleep, they marry in their sleep, they breed children in their sleep, they die in their sleep without ever waking up. They never understand the loveliness and the beauty of this thing that we call human existence.

(de Mello, p. 5)

He goes on to add that all mystics are unanimous in telling us that all is well. 'Though everything is a mess, all is well. Strange paradox, to be sure. But, tragically, most people never get to see that all is well because they are asleep. They are having a nightmare.' Personally, I would hesitate to claim with any degree of authority that most people remain in the state described above by de Mello for their entire lives, although I have no intention of disputing what he says. I simply do not know. I am certainly inclined to think, however, that most of us experience a good deal of difficulty in waking up to reality. In practice, saying this is much the same as saying that we have difficulty in really hearing the good news, in properly absorbing the implications of the declaration that the kingdom of God is here, now. Indeed, is this really very different from Teresa of Avila's assertion that many of us live on the periphery of ourselves – in the courtyards of our castles? To really live, and to attain understanding that lies beyond understanding, we have to enter into mystery. And reality – God's reality – is ultimately mystery.

Anthony Bloom approaches the problem in a rather different way in a discussion about what people often perceive to be the absence of God when they are praying. He talks about the problem of not realising we are outside the kingdom. In this state of unawareness, we may imagine that we are, in fact, within it, and we may well behave as though this were the case, 'never reaching that depth where the kingdom of God unfolds itself in all its beauty, its truth and its glory'. Having said this, he adds that he does not, in practice, envisage our being necessarily either in or out in a radical sense. He talks rather about progression 'from depth to depth, from height to height', a movement from a situation of richness and depth to one of greater richness and depth. Even when we are outside, he says, 'we are extraordinarily rich'. Indeed, it is because we have such rich lives that we may be misled into believing that we are fulfilled (Bloom, p. 13). The connection with poverty of spirit here is obvious. Only in true detachment from possessions can we gain true wealth. 'Blessed are the poor in spirit; for theirs *is* the kingdom of heaven' (Mt 5:3. Emphasis mine).

If, however, we remain oblivious to all of this, if, as de Mello might put it, we continue to sleepwalk our way through life, we will miss what would otherwise be obvious. We will go on searching for God only where we and others like us have decided that God is going to be. Many people say, for instance, that they see the hand of God in those extraordinary events that some of us call miracles, but what exactly do they mean when they say that? Has their awareness of a particular event that they have called a miracle really brought about a significant awakening in them? Do they now see things differently from the way they saw them before the event took place? Perhaps calling it a miracle has merely had the effect of helping them to remain, spiritually, precisely where they were before the event occurred. Indeed, perhaps the real reason why they are inclined to regard this particular event as a miracle is the fact that it appears to support the convictions they have long held about God. In other words, perhaps the event (or their interpretation of it) supports their world view and their vision of how God fits into that world view. If this were indeed the case, this could amount to a decidedly unhealthy state of affairs, one which would seem to have a good deal of similarity to that of many people who do not see the hand of God in anything at all. Reality would be passing them by. They would be unaware of it. In a sense, they would be living in an unreal world, a world that had largely been invented by themselves, although probably with the assistance of many other people.

The problem of unawareness manifests itself in other ways. Take, for example, the role of curiosity. Now, curiosity is, of course, not always bad. In fact, throughout human history, it has often played a positive role. For example, it has had a large part to play in many of the more useful endeavours of human beings, including advances in the sciences. It has urged people on to various important discoveries, breakthroughs and inventions. In many other kinds of cases in which curiosity is involved, however, its satisfaction, while not always harmful, tends to lead to very little of any import in our lives. If we turn to the role that it sometimes plays where miracles are concerned, for example, we see that some people may well be interested in finding out as much as they can about what exactly happened in a particular case. As a result of what they discover from other people – perhaps even witnesses to the event which they deem to be miraculous – they may experience profound emotions, and interesting thoughts may occur to them. As to whether or not something deeper and more significant happens to them, however, much depends upon whether or not, as de Mello might put it, they are spiritually awake. Incidentally, much the same can be said in regard to the reading of books about prayer and spirituality. In the first chapter, reference was made to the fact that the author of *The Cloud of Unknowing* discouraged his disciple from showing it to all and sundry. He refers specifically, along with other categories of people, to those who are merely curious, saying that, educated or uneducated, he does not wish them to be concerned with his book (*Cloud*, p. 12).

Those of us who find it difficult to accept what has been said about our tendency to sleepwalk our way through life need only reflect upon what the four evangelists have told us. It seems that a lot of the people who actually met Jesus of Nazareth, who spoke to him, heard what he said, and perhaps even touched him did not wake up. If they were, in this sense, asleep, of course, any statement to the effect that they really did hear what he said needs modification. We might say that they heard but did not hear, and saw, but did not see. They were, in a sense, sleepwalking when they met him. And so, they did not have faith in him. They did not trust him. They did not see the kingdom that he announced to them and discussed with them. They stayed, it seems, in their own little worlds, in their comfort zones. If things were so with them, is it so strange to suggest that something similar might have happened to many of us? At various points in our lives, we have surely all heard but not heard, read simple words but not really understood, and, of course, been largely unaware of the Holy Spirit in people we have met.

Clearly, in speaking of being awake or aware, de Mello is not telling us that we would benefit from a cold shower or a strong cup of coffee. Such procedures may or may not be of assistance where certain intellectual pursuits are concerned, but, as should be abundantly clear by now, merely intellectual pursuits are not our subject here. Becoming spiritually aware is something that happens to us. We just have to let it happen. We just have to let God be God in our lives. We have to trust the mystery.

> You don't change yourself; it's not *me* changing *me*. Change takes place *through* you, in you. That's about the most adequate way I can express it. You see change take place in you, through you; in your awareness, it happens. *You* don't do it. When you're doing it, it's a bad sign; it won't last. And if it does last, God have mercy on the people you're living with, because you're going to be very rigid. People who are converted on the basis of self-hatred and self-dissatisfaction are impossible to live with. Somebody said, 'If you want to be a martyr, marry a saint.' But in awareness, you keep your softness, your subtleness, your gentleness, your openness, your flexibility, and you don't push, change occurs.
>
> (de Mello, p. 167. Emphases his)

If we succeed in waking up, it seems that it will matter little whether we witness the kind of extraordinary events that tend to be regarded as 'miracles' or just the so-called ordinary events of life. If we wake up, we will see that, in reality, miracles are all around us. Our mysterious God is all around us, and everything speaks to us of the mystery that is God. Confining manifestations of the divine only to certain spheres is just one more way in which we try to make God fit into boxes or categories of our choosing, or even of our design – one more way, that is, in which we try to make God conform to the god that we have in mind, whatever that god may be. This takes us back to our discussion of St Paul in the first chapter. The Apostle to the Gentiles, we noted, refers to the fact that we can see God in creation. There would seem to be a certain awakening involved in such a process. It is surely much more than a mere intellectual exercise. When we become aware of God in creation, a personal encounter of some sort happens. One imagines, however, that the depth of awareness of the encounter varies from one person to another. Not all of us, it seems, see creation in quite the same light as Francis of Assisi saw it. Perhaps we could say that the depth of enlightenment varies.

People who wake up, of course, have a tendency to nod off again, and that tendency, it seems to me, shows its head not only when we have to deal with the needs of tired bodies. Something similar, I think, can happen in the spiritual life. We should never be disheartened, however, if we lose some of our awareness for a while now and then, and even fall back into some of our old ways of hiding God. Those old ways are never quite as effective as we tend to think they are. In fact, in the spiritual life, things are unlikely to happen in quite the way we expect. Even open rejection of God can prove to be ineffective. We need only think back to the experience of Anthony Bloom to which reference was made earlier in this chapter. He was an atheist, and expected nothing good to emerge from reading St Mark's gospel. Then, in a flash, he was aware of Christ. St Paul, on the other hand, was certainly no atheist when he set out on the road to Damascus, but his presence among the ranks of the Pharisees and his intolerance of Christianity appear to indicate a man who had definite ideas about God. The impression we gain from the text is that he had his god in a box of his own and others' making. In that sense, perhaps, he had more in common with a good many of us than did Bloom. In his case too, however, everything changed rather suddenly. In short, the mysterious God can break through the most formidable of defences. The kingdom really is here, now, and different miracles make different people aware of it.

The fair-haired man in the long, dark overcoat moved quietly from the centre of the church to his favourite spot in a quiet little alcove on the right. He settled himself into a comfortable position and waited. God, he knew, would do the rest.

Bibliography

St Ambrose, *De nabute*.

Anon.,*The Cloud of Unknowing and Other Works*, 2001, translated by A.C. Spearing, London: Penguin Books.

Aquinas, Thomas, *Summa Theologiae*.

Bloom, Anthony, *School for Prayer*, 1972, London: Libra Books.

Burrows, Ruth, *The Spiritual Teaching of St John of the Cross*, 1987, London: Darton, Longman and Todd.

Clement of Alexandria, *Who Is the Rich Man that Can Be Saved?*

Chrysostom, St John, 'Second Discourse on Lazarus and the Rich Man'.

Gorringe, T.J., *Capital and the Kingdom: Theological Ethics and Economic Order*, 1994, London, SPCK.

Gregory of Nyssa, *The Life of Moses*, 2006, New York, HarperCollins.

Heaps, John, *A Love that Dares to Question: A Bishop Challenges His Church*, 1998, Richmond: Aurora Books.

St Hilary, *Treatise on the Psalms*.

John Paul II, *Laborem exercens*, 1981.

Julian of Norwich, *Showings*, 1978, translated by Edmund Colledge and James Walsh, Mahwah, N.J.: Paulist.

de Mello, Anthony, *Awareness*, 1990, Grand Rapids: Zondervan.

Merton, Thomas, *Conjectures of a Guilty Bystander*, 1968, London: Burns & Oates.

Nolan, Albert, 'Face to Face with Mystery in Science and Religion' in Cornel W. Du Toit (ed.), *The Impact of Knowledge Systems on Human Development in Africa*, 2007, Pretoria: University of South Africa.

O'Leary, Donal, 'Begin with the Heart – Evangelizing as Humanizing' in *The Furrow*, 2007, Vol. 58.

Pseudo-Dyonisius, *Mystical Theology*.

Robinson, Geoffrey, *Confronting Power and Sex in the Catholic Church: Reclaiming the Spirit of Jesus*, 2007, Mulgrave, John Garratt.

Rohr, Richard, *Everything Belongs: The Gift of Contemplative Prayer*, 1999, New York: Crossroad.

Rohr, Richard, 'My Problem with Religion' in *The Pastoral Review*, 2006, Vol. 2, Issue 2.

Teresa of Avila, *Interior Castle*.

Teresa of Avila, *The Collected Works of St Teresa of Avila*, 1980, Vol. 2, translated by Kieran Kavanaugh and Otilio Rodriguez, Washington D. C.: ICS Publications.

Weil, Simone, *Letter to a Priest*, 1953, London: Routledge and Kegan Paul.

Wesley, John, 'The Almost Christian' in *Sermons on Several Occasions*, 1956, Worcester: The Epworth Press.

Notes

1 The mind, of course, does not have an eye. This particular metaphor, however, seems to be less problematic in this context, and the main point, I think, is well made.

2 Judaism and Islam, along with Christianity, are often described as Abrahamic faiths.

3 Luke, of course, wrote in Greek, and some scholars argue that the Greek word here translated as 'fear' could be translated as 'reverence', even if we were to discount the probable impact of Old Testament teachings upon the evangelist.

4 This is the translation in the New International Version, 1984 and today's New International Version. The Jerusalem Bible has: 'You trust in God, trust also in me'. The Revised Standard Version and the New Revised Standard Version, on the other hand opt for 'believe' instead of 'trust'.

5 John the Baptist is recorded as saying much the same thing at Mt 3:2.

6 This is taken from Julian's short text. The longer text has slightly different wording, but the same point is made.

7 Although Jesus may well have spoken in Greek at times, it seems likely that, on most of the occasions on which he spoke about the kingdom, he spoke in Aramaic.

8 It is well known that some of Jesus' contemporaries had been hoping that the messiah (the one specially anointed by God to bring salvation to Israel) would be a great king. It seems that they reasoned along these lines: 'If Jesus of Nazareth really is the messiah, he will become a magnificent sovereign in the vein of King David or Solomon, and

he will send the Romans away.' Given this state of affairs, it is easy to see how Jesus might have come across to them as one enormous disappointment when he talked about something that was much more spiritual, while making use of the same kind of regal terminology that they were using.

9   Matthew usually employs the phrase 'kingdom of heaven', whereas the other evangelists refer to the 'kingdom of God'.